Forensic Psychiatry

Essential Board Review

Forensic Psychiatry

Essential Board Review

Helen Mavourneen Farrell, M.D.

Forensic Psychiatrist
Instructor, Harvard Medical School
Staff Psychiatrist, Beth Israel Deaconess Medical Center

CRC Press
Taylor & Francis Group
Boca Raton London New York

CRC Press is an imprint of the
Taylor & Francis Group, an **informa** business

CRC Press
Taylor & Francis Group
6000 Broken Sound Parkway NW, Suite 300
Boca Raton, FL 33487-2742

Printed on acid-free paper
Version Date: 20150303

International Standard Book Number-13: 978-1-4987-1609-3 (Paperback)

Visit the Taylor & Francis Web site at
http://www.taylorandfrancis.com

and the CRC Press Web site at
http://www.crcpress.com

For my parents,
thank you for all of your love and support.

Contents

Section 4: Board-style questions

Introduction

Forensic psychiatry is a board certified specialty recognized by the American Board of Psychiatry and Neurology (ABPN). Certification into this esteemed specialty requires a medical degree, successful completion of an accredited four-year psychiatry residency training program, graduation from a one-year intensive and accredited forensic psychiatry fellowship training program, and passage of the forensic psychiatry certification examination.

This process is both thrilling and challenging at once. There is significant depth to the principles, frameworks, and cases that comprise mental health law. Understanding all of this is a requirement for competency in forensics and is vigorously tested on the certification examination.

The idea for this book came out of my own experiences with forensic board preparation. During my studies, I wished for a concise and efficient study aid. I wanted something that would complement the detailed information provided within the numerous forensic psychiatry textbooks, not to mention the three-day intensive American Academy of Psychiatry and the Law (AAPL) Forensic Psychiatry Review Course. These remain, in my opinion, the most thorough resources for forensic psychiatry knowledge.

Forensic Psychiatry: Essential Board Review was developed in the spirit of mentoring trainees who seek a career in forensics. As the title suggests, this is a review book and not meant to be a far-reaching or detailed analysis of the material content required for competency in forensic psychiatry. The book is a concise and practical tool recommended for quick revision, rote memorization, and self-assessment of knowledge. The board-style questions are to be used for guidance only and are not representative of the actual exam questions. Used as an aid to other texts, journals, and review courses, this book can help learners maximize their knowledge although it in no way guarantees their outcome on the board examination or beyond.

A large audience can benefit from this book, which is the first of its kind. Although this was developed primarily for forensic psychiatrists, it will also be useful to psychologists, social workers, criminologists, mental health law attorneys, general psychiatrists, medical students, and anyone else curious about mental health and the law.

Forensic Psychiatry: Essential Board Review is arranged into four sections. Section 1, Board Examination Tips and Pitfalls, offers readers sage advice on everything from registering for the examination, to effective studying techniques, to the powers of embracing a positive attitude.

Section 2, High-Yield Notes, provides a broad review of some of the important topics in forensic psychiatry. Some of the subjects touched upon here include forensic ethics, civil and criminal issues, and other special issues in forensic psychiatry. In Section 3, Legal Cases, there is a concise review of many of the important mental health legal cases. In an effort to parallel the content sections of the ABPN Forensic Psychiatry Examination, the cases are broken into eight chapters: Legal Regulation of Psychiatry; Civil; Criminal; Death Penalty; Corrections/Correctional Healthcare; Legal Systems/Basic Law; Children and Families; and Special Issues.

Section 4, Board-Style Questions, comprises the bulk of this book. Reflecting the importance of self-assessments during the review process, there are over 100 board-style questions along with answers and detailed explanations.

At the heart of this book is my passion for education. I ultimately pursued a career in forensic psychiatry because I knew that gaining a better understanding of mental health law would make me a better physician, psychiatrist, and instructor. Whether you use this book as an introduction to forensic psychiatry, revision of key material, solidification of memory, rote memorization, or active self-assessment, I hope this serves as a helpful guide in your academic and career pursuits.

Author

Helen M. Farrell, M.D., is a forensic psychiatrist on staff at Beth Israel Deaconess Medical Center in Boston and an instructor in psychiatry at Harvard Medical School. Dr. Farrell has presented nationally to diverse groups including members of the American Psychiatric Association, the American Academy of Psychiatry and the Law, the American Academy of Forensic Sciences, and the American Bar Association. She has published widely in academic journals and books on the topics of psychiatry and forensic psychiatry. In addition, her work has appeared in *JAMA* and various media and newspaper outlets including *KevinMD.com, Psychology Today,* and the *New York Times.*

section 1

Board examination tips and pitfalls

As you get ready for the forensic psychiatry board examination, take a moment to be mindful of your feelings. What do you feel as you think about the task ahead?

- Excitement—This is a chance to showcase your knowledge and competency
- Burden—Feeling overwhelmed by the process of studying for yet another major certification examination while juggling everything else in your busy life
- Anxiety—Worry about failing the test, which could cause personal and professional embarrassment

If you're like most people, then probably all of the above resonate with you on some level. The key to having an enjoyable and successful outcome is to focus on the exam as a process and not just a day. This will help you maintain balance in your life and studies. Following these four principles of effective education helped me to be successful: proactivity, preparation, performance, and positivity.

chapter one

Proactivity

Being proactive in the exam process is vital. Not only does it serve to reduce anxiety—an unavoidable trait of most test-takers—but it also ensures that you will not get bogged down in the technicalities of the exam or incur unwanted costs. The more proactive you are, the more you will minimize the unavoidable and cumbersome hurdles commonly encountered by exam candidates.

Getting started

When should you take the exam? This is one of the most important questions for examinees. For your best results, I would emphasize the importance of taking the exam as soon as you are eligible. Following a rigorous forensic training program, you will most likely enter a career where the bulk of your daily practice will be non-forensic in nature. This distance will be compounded by your hectic schedule building a practice, juggling academic pursuits, and maintaining a work–life balance.

The American Board of Psychiatry and Neurology (ABPN) offers the initial forensic psychiatry board exam every two years, thereby putting distance between you and the complex material content. The longer you are away from the material, the easier it is to forget it. You will certainly have better recall of the didactic material soon after you have learned it.

Registering

Once you have settled on a year to take the exam, you need to register. When it comes to where you take the examination, I recommend choosing someplace local. All candidates will need to complete and submit an application in order to qualify and apply for an examination. The ABPN accepts and actually requests applications for the forensic board examination well in advance of the testing date. Be sure to check its website for application materials at http://www.abpn.com/ifas_fp.html.

Late applications are accepted up to a certain point, but they come with a significantly increased fee. Each application will be reviewed by the credentials department. Tables 1.1 and 1.2 summarize the 2015 timeline and prices for the Initial Certification and Maintenance of Certification Examinations as made available by the ABPN website http://www.abpn.com/sub_fp.html.

Table 1.1 Initial Certification Examination

Applications available	January 5, 2015
Deadline	April 1, 2015
Late application deadline	June 1, 2015
Application fee	$700
Examination fee	$1200
Late application fee	$500
Admission materials e-mailed	August 3, 2015
Choices of test dates	October 13–16, 2015

Table 1.2 Maintenance of Certification Examination

Applications available	August 4, 2014
Deadline	November 3, 2014
Late application deadline	December 1, 2014
Application fee	$700
Examination fee	$800
Late application fee	$500
Admission materials e-mailed	February 2, 2015
Choices of test dates	April 13–17, 2015

In summary, when it comes to being proactive be sure to:

- Commit to a testing year and date
- Choose a testing center that is near you
- Register for the exam well in advance to avoid paying a pricey late fee
- Secure with your employer that you can have the test date free from work
- Start preparing for the exam

chapter two

Preparation

Now an avid runner, I went from couch to half-marathon several years ago. The key to my successful race-day run was that I started early and made running a part of my daily routine. The same principle applies for the boards. It's not just a day, it's a process that requires several months of daily structure, commitment, and endurance.

After years of medical school, residency training, and beyond, you have undoubtedly honed and mastered the skills necessary to diagnose and treat patients, not to mention pass your exams. This is not a time to change your proven successful habits. The forensic psychiatric examination, however, is a very different type of exam that tests material that you might not be employing in everyday practice.

Scoping the task

There are several things you can do to maximize your score on the board examination. The first, of course, is to know the material as well as you can. If you are like most forensic psychiatrists, the bulk of your practice is not forensic in nature. This can make recall of detailed cases, confusing law, and general issues difficult to recall. At this point in life, you are probably juggling many time consuming things. Work is undoubtedly busy and you also have relationships to cultivate and maintain with friends and family. Do not let the exam become an overwhelming factor in your already busy life. Prepare early and you will find yourself in a relaxed state of revision come one to two months before the exam.

Needless to say, passing the boards requires a broad knowledge of the tested content. Scoping out the task will help you feel in control of the process ahead. The American Board of Psychiatry and Neurology (ABPN) focuses on eight main areas for the forensic examination:

- Legal regulation of psychiatry
- Civil
- Criminal
- Death penalty
- Corrections
- Legal systems/basic law
- Children and families
- Special issues

The bulk of the material seems to be weighted on legal regulation, civil and criminal issues, and basic law. Although all areas are important, adjust your revision accordingly. In-depth knowledge about minutiae involving the death penalty with a shallow understanding of civil forensic psychiatry, for example, will not pay off.

Strategize

A successful exam score is attainable and possible. It relies mostly on preparation. The way I approached my boards was through early detailed revision of resources including textbooks, review courses, meetings, presentation notes, medical journals, and forensic psychiatry journals.

Daily review became a seamless part of my day for months before the exam. Finding support through others helped me accomplish this. I talked with my colleagues, studied with other candidates, and found that sharing the experience made it easier and more enjoyable.

Board-style questions

Self-assessment exam questions are another useful study tool. Some residency programs now require completion of self-assessment modules as part of a maintenance of certification program. Completing self-assessment modules during training is associated with demonstrable improvement in certification exam results.

Revision is one of the most personal and individualized processes within academic life. Learners have different sets of knowledge, varying revision techniques, and distinct psychological and life contexts into which to fit the revision.

Completing board-style questions can help you be attentive to your own personal strengths and weaknesses. If there is a specific topic you struggle with, then take a break from doing questions and modify your plan.

Monitoring your experiences and aptitude early in the process will make it possible to modify your revision timetable for the remaining time so that it works most effectively for you.

Here are some tips to maximize your score:

- Know the material well
- Start preparing well in advance
- Know what types of questions will be asked
- Understand how the test will be scored
- Use your time efficiently
- Relax and enjoy

chapter three

Performance

You're finally ready for the big day! This test is an opportunity to showcase your mastery of the complexities of psychiatry and the law. Be sure to get enough sleep and approach the exam with ample energy. When you are waiting to go into the exam room there is no point looking backward over what you haven't covered, what you never understood, or what you thought you'd learned but can't seem to remember. All you can influence now is the future. You are where you are and now you have to make the best of what you've got.

Answering questions

The American Board of Psychiatry and Neurology (ABPN) scores the forensic psychiatry board exam by crediting correct answers. There is no penalty for getting a question wrong, so answer everything. It pays to guess!

Narrow choices as best as you can and read the questions carefully looking for key words such as *never* and *always*, and *except*. The test is multiple choice. Even if "A" seems to be the right answer, look over the other questions too. Try not to change answers. Your first guess is usually right. Change an answer only if you are certain that your initial choice was incorrect.

Use your time effectively. Since each question counts the same, if one is too difficult to be answered in a reasonable amount of time, make an educated guess at the answer immediately and make a note to go back to it for further work after you have finished the rest of the test. Do not spend too much time on any one question. If you don't pace yourself and have to randomly guess, your score will suffer.

Follow these tips on exam day:

- Get enough sleep the night before the exam.
- Wear comfortable clothing to the examination.
- Arrive early enough to sign in and get your entire allotted time for the exam.
- Check the test information to be certain that you bring all needed materials (i.e., receipt of registration, identification). Do not be caught

short by failing to bring your picture ID or the registration receipt with you to the testing center.

- Bring a snack and utilize break times to recharge.
- Be familiar with the test format so you don't waste time trying to figure it out.

chapter four

Positivity

As you have probably noticed, the bulk of this section has been focused on what you can do to pass your exam. This is because a positive attitude is absolutely key!

Needless to say, skipping any of the recommendations, failing to study, relying on only one study aid, neglecting board-style questions, or succumbing to anxiety on the test day will all lead to poor results.

In addition to a passing score, another goal you might want to consider is to prevent burnout from the boards. Do not let this examination consume your life. Good self-care and preservation of your physical and mental well-being during the testing season are just as important as a passing score. Be sure to get plenty of rest, maintain a healthy eating and exercise schedule, share time with your loved ones, and remain focused at your place of employment. Attend to any mental health needs that you might have and reach out for support.

Mental preparation is vital to success. Most people are familiar with pretest anxiety. But butterflies, sweaty palms, and fear do not have to overcome you. You merely need to steady yourself. The trick is to do everything as normally as possible both during your revision course and on exam day.

Keep a positive attitude and avoid these common pitfalls:

- Neglecting to use pedagogical aids (i.e., board-style questions)
- Getting bogged down in minute details of low-yield topics
- Trying to master every topic in forensics
- Putting aside your personal needs during the revision process
- Studying with a friend where you spend more time chatting than working
- Registering late
- Arriving at the testing center late
- Panicking on test day
- Failing to utilize breaks during the exam
- Forgetting to pack a sweater for the test
- Scheduling work after the exam (this will leave you feeling rushed during the exam)
- Being anything other than positive

section 2

High-yield notes

chapter five

Overview

Ethical guidelines

Forensic psychiatrists are held to standards that fall under four realms.

- Confidentiality
- Consent
- Honesty and striving for objectivity
- Qualifications

U.S. Constitutional amendments 1–14

First	Prohibits the making of any law respecting an establishment of religion, impeding the free exercise of religion, abridging the freedom of speech, infringing on the freedom of the press, interfering with the right to peaceably assemble or prohibiting the petitioning for a governmental redress of grievances.
Second	Protects the right to keep and bear arms.
Third	Prohibits quartering of soldiers in private homes without the owner's consent during peacetime.
Fourth	Prohibits unreasonable searches and seizures, and sets out requirements for search warrants based on probable cause as determined by a neutral judge or magistrate.
Fifth	Sets out rules for indictment by grand jury and eminent domain, protects the right to due process, and prohibits self-incrimination and double jeopardy. Protects the right to a fair and speedy public trial by jury, including the rights to be notified of the accusations, to confront the accuser, to obtain witnesses and to retain counsel.
Sixth	Provides for the right to a fair and speedy trial by jury in certain civil cases, according to common law. Provides the right to face an accuser.
Seventh	Provides for the right to trial by jury in certain civil cases, according to common law.
Eighth	Prohibits excessive fines and excessive bail, as well as cruel and unusual punishment.
Ninth	Protects rights not enumerated in the Constitution.

Tenth	Reinforces the principle of federalism by stating that the federal government possesses only those powers delegated to it by the states or the people through the Constitution.
Eleventh	Makes states immune from suits from out-of-state citizens and foreigners not living within the state borders; lays the foundation for sovereign immunity.
Twelfth	Revises presidential election procedures.
Thirteenth	Abolishes slavery, and involuntary servitude, except as punishment for a crime.
Fourteenth	Defines citizenship, contains the Privileges or Immunities Clause, the Due Process Clause, the Equal Protection Clause, and deals with post-Civil War issues.

Why a patient's psychiatrist cannot be their expert

- Clinical, ethical, and legal incompatibilities.
- There is a lack of warnings in the clinical role.
- Testimony could actually harm the examinee/patient.
- Clinical focus of treatment is bias.

Standards of proof

Reason to believe	Lowest
Probable cause	<50%
Preponderance of the evidence	51%
Clear and convincing	70–80%
Beyond a reasonable doubt	>90%

Principles of psychiatric-legal report writing

- Clarity
- Simplicity
- Brevity
- Humanity

chapter six

Civil

Experts are often sought for opinions in a number of different civil areas of the law. Examples of competencies in civil law:

- Guardianship
- Competency to make treatment decisions
- Competency to consent to research
- Testamentary capacity
- Worker's compensation

Disability

Disability is the inability to engage in any substantial gainful act, due to an impairment that could lead to death or have lasting consequences more than 12 months.

Social security disability insurance (SSDI)

- There must be a medically determinable impairment.
- The impairment must result in an inability to work.
- Inability to perform work means an inability to perform any work available in substantial numbers in the national economy.
- Consideration may be given to age, education, or previous work, in addition to medical factors.
- Pays benefits to workers who have qualified for coverage (by working) and who have become disabled.

Supplemental security income (SSI)

Supplemental Security Income (SSI) is a social welfare program designed to provide income support for people who have become disabled regardless of whether they have ever worked.

Mental disorders

Disorders that qualify as mental disorders for adults by the Social Security Administration:

- Organic mental disorders
- Psychotic disorders
- Affective disorders
- Mental retardation
- Anxiety-related disorders
- Somatoform disorders
- Personality disorders
- Substance addiction disorders
- Autistic and other pervasive developmental disorders

Disorders that qualify as mental disorders for children by the Social Security Administration:

- Organic mental disorders
- Psychotic disorders
- Affective disorders
- Mental retardation
- Anxiety-related disorders
- Somatoform disorders
- Personality disorders
- Autistic and other pervasive developmental disorders
- Attention deficit hyperactivity disorder
- Developmental and emotional disorders of newborn and younger infants

Tests of functional limitations that qualify for disability:

- Activities of daily living
- Social functioning
- Concentration/persistence/pace
- Frequent episodes of decompensation

Requirements for capacity to make treatment decisions:

- Ability to express a choice about treatment
- Ability to understand information relevant to the treatment decision
- Ability to appreciate the significance of that treatment information for one's own situation
- Ability to reason with relevant information in a logical process of weighing treatment options

Workers' compensation law

Workers' compensation law is an alternative system to sue under tort law. There are three types of mental stress claims in worker's compensation as outlined in Table 6.1.

Table 6.1 Mental Stress Claims Allowable in Workers' Compensation Law

Physical–Mental	Trauma → physical injury → mental disorder
Mental–Physical	Mental stimulation → physical injury (i.e., stress leading to heart attack)
Mental–Mental	Mental stimulation → mental disorder (i.e., stress leading to panic attack)

- Standard = Preponderance of the evidence
- Administrative decision
- Fixed portion is given for lost wages

Prior to workers' compensation law, employers had three major defenses:

- Contributory negligence
- Assumption of risk
- Fellow servant rule

Torts of emotional distress

1. Intentional infliction of emotional distress (IIED)

"Tort of outrage"—Objective standard (what a reasonable person would find "outrageous")
Plaintiff has the burden of proof to show:

- Defendant acted intentionally/recklessly
- Conduct was extreme and dangerous
- Conduct caused emotional distress for victim
- Emotional distress on the victim was severe

2. Negligent infliction of emotional distress (NIED). Most common tort of emotional distress.

chapter seven

Criminal

Forensic psychiatrists frequently serve as experts in courts of law at different levels of legal action when there is a question of the relationship between mental states and crimes. Knowledge of penological systems and correctional institutions is therefore important and these topics are reviewed in Tables 7.1 and 7.2.

Table 7.1 Evolvement of the Penological System

Pennsylvania System, 1790	Punishment cells (i.e., solitary confinement)
Reformatory Model, 1870–1900	Prisoners were given trade work
Progressive Era, 1950–1970	Rehabilitation was implemented in institutions

Prisoners

Facts about prisoners:

- The most common diagnosis in a correctional setting is substance use.
- The most common mechanism of suicide in a correctional setting is by hanging.

Table 7.2 Correctional Institutions and Suicide Risk

Lockup	• Most common correctional setting
	• Most common site of suicides
	• The highest risk time for a suicide in this setting is within 24 hours
	• Suicide victims are young white men
Jail	• Suicide is the second most common cause of death here
	• Men commit suicide in jail > women
	• The highest risk time for a suicide to occur in a prison is within the first year of incarceration
	• Ages at risk are <18 years old and >55 years old
Prison	• Suicide risk is equal for men and women
	• White inmates are at high risk for suicide
	• Suicides occur within the first year
	• The biggest risk factor for suicide is bad news

The United States Supreme Court has recognized these constitutional rights for prisoners:

- Right to marry
- Right to freedom of speech
- Right to religious freedom
- Right to have access to courts
- Right to equal protection of the law
- Right to due process
- Right not to be subjected to cruel and unusual punishment

The United States Supreme Court has not granted prisoners the following:

- Right to vote
- Right to drug and alcohol treatment
- Right to procreate

Competency to stand trial

The Dusky Standard of Competence states that a defendant is incompetent to stand trial if he is unable to understand the trial's nature and objectives or unable to assist in his own defense.

The "nature and objectives" of a trial include:

- Charges against the defendant
- Severity of the charges
- Pleas that may be entered
- Roles of courtroom personnel
- The trial's adversarial nature

"Assisting in one's own defense" includes the ability to:

- Work with attorney
- Appreciate defendant's role
- Understand plea bargaining
- Make rational defense decisions
- Consider using mental illness defenses
- Pay attention in court
- Be free of self-defeating behavior
- Evaluate evidence and predict probable trial outcome
- Display appropriate behavior
- Give reliable account of offense

Common reasons defendants are found incompetent to stand trial are:

- Low intelligence or dementia impairs understanding the trial process
- Depression and self-defeating behavior limit motivation for trial's best outcome
- Mania impairs ability to act appropriately in courtroom
- Paranoid delusions impair ability to work with defense counsel
- Disorganized thinking impairs concentration and attention
- Delusions, disorganized thinking, low intellect, or dementia result in irrational decision-making about defense
- Hallucinations distract from paying attention to the trial

Insanity

The insanity defense is rarely sought and has a very low success rate when raised as a defense in court.

The definition of insanity has evolved over centuries, as outlined in Table 7.3, and is considered to be distinct from merely a diagnosis of psychosis.

Signs that a defendant knew an act was wrong and therefore go against a defense of insanity:

1. Efforts to avoid detection
    - Wearing gloves or a mask during the offense
    - Concealing the weapon
    - Falsifying information
    - Committing the act in the dark

Table 7.3 Insanity Defense Timeline

Year	Standard	Description
1724	Wild Beast	A total deprivation of memory and understanding
1840	Irresistible Impulse	"some controlling disease … was the acting power within him which he could not resist"
1843	M'Naghten Rule	The defendant did not know the nature/ quality or wrongfulness of the offense
1955	American Law Institute's Model Penal Code	Combined M'Naghten Rule with irresistible impulse standard
1984	Federal Insanity Defense Reform Act	Dropped the irresistible impulse standard after attempted assassination of President Reagan

2. Disposal of evidence
   - Washing away blood
   - Removing fingerprints
   - Discarding the weapon
   - Hiding the body
3. Efforts to avoid apprehension
   - Fleeing
   - Lying to authorities

Examples of criminal competencies:

- Competence to waive Miranda rights/to confess
- Competence to testify in criminal matters
- Competence to stand trial
- Competence to refuse an insanity defense
- Competence to waive right to counsel
- Competence to plead guilty
- Competence to be sentenced
- Competence to be executed

chapter eight

Special issues

Recklessness

There are two forms of recklessness:

- Subjective recklessness—A person knows and is aware of a situation that he/she disregards
- Objective recklessness—The risk of harm is so high that the person should have known that harm would result

Competence for execution

The United States Supreme Court case of *Ford v. Wainwright* established several rationales for why a person must be competent for execution:

- An incompetent person might be unable to provide counsel with last-minute information leading to vacation of the sentence.
- Madness is punishment in itself.
- An incompetent person cannot make peace with God.
- Execution of an incompetent person has no deterrent effect on the population.
- In the Court ruling they actually referred to execution of the incompetent as a "miserable spectacle."
- Retribution cannot be exacted from an incompetent person.

Child maltreatment

The major types of child maltreatment are:

- Neglect
- Physical
- Sexual
- Emotional

Juvenile justice and delinquency prevention act

The Juvenile Justice and Delinquency Prevention Act of 1974:

- Established the office of Juvenile Justice and Delinquency Prevention
- Emphasized community-based treatment

- Resulted in deinstitutionalization of status offenders
- Limits placements of juveniles in adult institutions

Malingering

Malingering is the purposeful production of falsely or grossly exaggerated complaints with the secondary goal of receiving some reward. Tables 8.1 and 8.2 describe signs of and diagnostic tests for malingering.

Table 8.1 Signs of Malingering

Understandable motive to malinger

Marked variability of presentation as evidenced by:
- Marked discrepancies in interview and noninterview behaviors
- Gross inconsistencies in reported psychotic symptoms
- Blatant contradictions between reported prior episodes and documented psychiatric history

Improbable psychiatric symptoms:
- Reporting elaborate psychotic symptoms that lack common paranoid, grandiose, or religious themes
- Sudden emergence of purported symptoms to explain antisocial behaviors
- Atypical hallucinations and delusions

Confirmation of malingering by:
- Admission of malingering following confrontation
- Presence of strong corroborative information, such as psychometric data or history

Table 8.2 Diagnostic Tests for Malingering

MMPI-2	Minnesota Multiphasic Personality Inventory–2
PAI	Personality Assessment Inventory
SIRS	Structured Interview of Reported Symptoms
M-FAST	Miller Forensic Assessment of Symptoms Test
TOMM	Test of Memory Malingering
PDRT	Portland Digit Recognition Test
VSVT	Victoria Symptoms Validity Test
WMT	Word Memory Test

section 3

Legal cases

chapter nine

Legal regulation of psychiatry

Confidentiality and privilege

Case

In Re Lifschutz, 2 Cal. 3d 415, 467 P.2d 557 (1970)

Issue
Psychotherapist–patient privilege

Summary
Joseph Housek had filed a civil suit for damages in a California court. He alleged that from injuries sustained as the victim of an assault, he had pain, suffering, and emotional distress. Dr. Lifschutz, a psychotherapist, who was later called to testify, treated these symptoms. Dr. Lifschutz invoked privilege, and he refused to produce medical records or answer questions.

Holding
It is the patient and not the psychotherapist who has a constitutional right to privacy. Privilege in treatment belongs to the patient and not to the doctor. Dr. Lifschutz was in contempt of court.

Case

Whalen v. Roe, 429 U.S. 589, 97 S.Ct. 869 (1977)

Issue
Controlled substances and right to privacy

Summary
New York's Controlled Substances Act aimed to prevent the spread of prescription drugs into an illicit market. The act required all prescriptions for Schedule II drugs be written on an official triplicate form and stored. Four identifying criteria were required on each form. The prescribing physician, the dispensing pharmacy, the drug and dose, and the name and address of the patient. The third copy of the form was to be forwarded to the Department of Health. Patients and doctors brought suit in federal court and claimed this Act would stigmatize patients as drug addicts.

Holding
The Act is a reasonable exercise of police powers. The Act could reasonably be expected to deter potential violators from illegitimately obtaining and using drugs.

Case

Doe v. Roe, 400 N.Y. Supp.2d 668 (1977)

Issue
Patient confidentiality

Summary
Dr. Jane Roe, a psychiatrist and her husband, Dr. Peter Roe, a psychologist, published a book describing the intimate details of their psychotherapeutic sessions with a former patient, Jane Doe. Ms. Doe filed suit claiming this was a breach of her privacy.

Holding
The court awarded damages of $20,000 and permanently barred the defendants from circulating or publishing the book.

Case

People v. Stritzinger, 34 Cal. 3d 505, 668 P.2d 738 (1983)

Issue
Psychotherapist–patient privilege and confidentiality

Summary
Carl Stritzinger was convicted of child molestation, including sexual acts with his 14-year-old stepdaughter, Sarah. When Sarah's mother found out, she arranged for Dr. Walker to meet with both Sarah and Carl. Dr. Walker first met with Sarah, who reported the sexual misconduct, prompting Dr. Walker's mandate to notify authorities. Later, Carl Stritzinger shared details of the sexual acts with Dr. Walker, information that the doctor later shared in his testimony. Stritzinger argued that his conviction was based on a violation of his psychotherapist–patient privilege.

Holding
The California Supreme Court acknowledged the psychotherapist–patient privilege as one grounded in the patient's right to privacy. There could be exceptions, however, such as a compelling state interest in detecting and

prosecuting child abuse. This was not one of those compelling exceptions, however, because Sarah had already disclosed the abuse, thereby triggering a report to authorities. Carl Stritzinger's privilege remained intact.

Case

State v. Andring, 342 N.W.2d 128 (Minn. 1984)

Issue
Privilege and group therapy

Summary
David Andring was charged in Minnesota with multiple counts of sexual misconduct. While out on bond and awaiting trial, Andring voluntarily sought help for depression and alcoholism at a psychiatric hospital. Andring participated in group therapy at the hospital, where he shared his experiences of sexual conduct with young girls. Prosecutors wanted the hospital records disclosed, but Andring argued that these should be protected under the federal Comprehensive Alcohol Abuse and Alcoholism Prevention, Treatment, and Rehabilitation Act.

Holding
The court recognized the benefits of group therapy and viewed sessions as an integral and necessary part of the patient's diagnosis and treatment. They held that a ruling which excluded group therapy from the scope of the psychotherapist–patient privilege would seriously limit its effectiveness.

Case

Jaffee v. Redmond, 116 S.Ct. 1923 (1996)

Issue
Therapist–patient privilege and social workers

Summary
Mary Lu Redmond, a police officer, shot and killed Ricky Allen while on duty in Illinois. This was a traumatic incident for Redmond who sought counseling from a social worker. Allen's family brought suit against Redmond alleging that she used excessive force in the killing of Allen. The prosecution wanted access to the social worker's therapy notes for use in the trial, but Redmond argued that these should be protected under her psychotherapist–patient privilege.

Holding

There is a psychotherapist–patient privilege that is protected from disclosure under the Federal Rules of Evidence 501. This privilege was extended to include not only psychiatrists and psychologists but also social workers.

Informed consent

Case

Canterbury v. Spence, 150 U.S. App. D.C. 263, 464 F.2d 772 (1972)

Issue

Informed consent and reasonable disclosure

Summary

Dr. Spence evaluated 19-year-old Jerry Canterbury for severe upper back pain and recommended surgery. Canterbury agreed without any questions. The surgery left Canterbury paralyzed and he filed suit claiming that Dr. Spence was negligent in his performance and his failure to inform Canterbury of the risks of the surgery.

Holding

Patients are in a fiduciary relationship with their physician. The physician is therefore under a duty to communicate information about abnormal findings, recommended treatments and alternatives, and any risks that may be involved in treatment. Since full disclosure is not reasonable, an objective standard should be used, one that considers what a prudent person in the patient's position would want to know.

Case

Kaimowitz v. Michigan DMH, 1 MDLR 147 (1976)

Issue

Informed consent and institutionalized persons

Summary

A man, Mr. Doe, was civilly committed to the state hospital as a criminal sexual psychopath after raping and murdering a student nurse. He was offered treatment via an experimental psychosurgery which might help to control his aggression. He consented to receive the experimental psychosurgery. A third party, Mr. Kaimowitz, became aware of this plan and notified the press. He then filed a writ of habeas corpus on behalf of Mr. Doe, alleging that he was being illegally detained for experimental surgery.

Holding

It is impossible to obtain truly voluntary informed consent from within an institution.

Case

Clites v. Iowa, 322 N.W. 2d 917 (Iowa Ct. App. 1982)

Issue

Informed consent and antipsychotic medications

Summary

Timothy Clites was mentally retarded and living at a state hospital. At 18 years old, he was prescribed antipsychotics and was restrained for aggression. Years later, Clites was diagnosed with tardive dyskinesia and his father submitted a claim for the negligent use of medications and physical restraints.

Holding

The tardive dyskinesia was induced by the negligent use of antipsychotics and the court found that since the condition was permanent, Clites should receive appropriate damages. The court awarded damages of over $700,000 for past and future medical expenses and pain and suffering. The hospital was guilty of nonstandard care and using medications not for the patient's benefit, but for the staff's convenience. This was the first appellate case affirming the need for informed consent to avoid paying for damages for tardive dyskinesia.

Duty to protect

Case

Tarasoff v. Regents, 17 Cal. 3d 425, 551 P.2d 334, 131 Cal. Rptr. 14 (1976)

Issue

Special relationships and duty

Summary

Prosenjit Poddar, a University of California, Berkeley student, had informed his psychologist of his intent to murder Tatiana Tarasoff when she returned home from vacation. The doctor notified the campus police, who took Poddar into custody but later found him to be rational and calm, so they released him without further investigation or evaluation at a hospital. Poddar later killed Tarasoff, and her parents filed a suit against the Regents of the University of california. The case was eventually appealed to the California Supreme Court.

Holding

The court found that a "special relationship" exists between therapists and patients. When a treater is made aware of an explicit risk of severe harm or death to a third party, he/she has a duty to that party.

Tarasoff I—Duty to warn
Tarasoff II—Duty to protect

Case

Lipari v. Sears, 497 F. Supp. 185 (D. Neb. 1980)

Issue

Duty to third parties

Summary

Ulysses Cribbs fired a shotgun in a nightclub in Omaha, Nebraska, killing Dennis Lipari and wounding Lipari's wife, Ruth. Ruth filed a wrongful death suit against Sears for negligence in selling a gun to Cribbs. Sears then filed a third-party complaint against the United States under the Federal Torts Claims Act, claiming that the Veterans Administration, where Cribbs was a patient, knew or should have known that Cribbs was dangerous.

Holding

The Court extended the duty to protect to third persons belonging to a class of foreseeable victims, rather than to a specifically identified individual.

Case

Jablonski v. U.S., 712 F.2d 391 (9th Cir. 1983)

Issue

Duty to protect

Summary

Dr. Kopiloff, a psychiatrist at the Loma Linda Veterans Administration (VA) Hospital, evaluated Phillip Jablonski, a man who had a history of imprisonment for rape. Dr. Kopiloff, knowing Jablonski had recently attempted rape, urged Jablonski to undergo a psychiatric admission for evaluation and treatment. Jablonski refused and Dr. Kopiloff did not have sufficient evidence at the time to commit the man involuntarily. Jablonski left the VA and proceeded to murder his wife's mother, Ms. Kimball.

Kimball's daughter, Meghan Jablonski, brought suit under the Federal Tort Claims Act for wrongful death of her mother resultant of negligence from the VA psychiatrist.

Holding

A therapist owes a duty to protect a foreseeable victim, even in the absence of a specific threat by a patient. The court concluded that the plaintiff met their burden of proof:

- A doctor–patient relationship existed
- The psychiatrist knew Mr. Jablonski was dangerous
- Ms. Kimball was an identified and foreseeable victim
- The psychiatrist did not take necessary steps to discharge his duty
- Hospital negligence proximately caused Ms. Kimball's death

Case

Naidu v. Laird, 539 A.2d 1064 (Del. 1988)

Issue

Foreseeable risk and duty to protect

Summary

Hilton Putney, a psychotic man, deliberately crashed his car into that of George Laird and killed him. Putney had recently been hospitalized and treated by Dr. Naidu five months prior to that fatal crash. Naidu felt compelled to discharge Putney because he was under a voluntary status and asked to leave. Mrs. Laird filed a wrongful death suit against the doctor, whom she claimed should have foreseen this risk.

Holding

Dr. Naidu had sufficient knowledge to be able to predict Putney's continuing dangerousness. The Supreme Court of Delaware concluded that Putney's desire to leave the hospital in no way obligated the doctor to release him when he posed a real threat to a third party.

Expert testimony

Case

Frye v. U.S., 293 F. 1013 (1923)

Issue

Expert testimony and admissibility

Summary

James Frye was convicted of murder. During the trial, the judge refused to hear testimony about the results of a lie detector test.

Holding

It is difficult to discern the point at which a scientific principle or discovery becomes demonstrable rather than experimental. At this point, lie detector tests had not gained sufficient standing and scientific recognition to justify its admission as expert testimony.

Case

Barefoot v. Estelle, 463 U.S. 880, 103 S.Ct. 3383 (1983)

Issue

Psychiatric testimony at criminal sentencing

Summary

Thomas Barefoot was convicted of murdering a police officer in Texas. At his sentencing hearing, Dr. James Grigson was called by the prosecution to testify about Barefoot's future dangerousness risk. Dr. Grigson had never evaluated Barefoot, but he did testify regarding hypothetical questions, which the defense contested.

Holding

Testimony on hypothetical questions is permissible, even if the doctor did not evaluate the offender, only if such questions relate to future dangerousness.

Case

Daubert v. Merrell Dow Pharmaceuticals, 61 U.S.L.S. 4805, 113 S.Ct. 2786 (1993)

Issue

Expert testimony and admissibility

Summary

Jason Daubert was born with serious birth defects which his parents claimed resulted from maternal ingestion of a drug from Merrell Dow Pharmaceuticals, Inc. The parents sued the pharmaceutical company.

Holding

The United States Supreme Court ruled that the Frye test had been superseded by the Federal Rules of Evidence. Rule 402 establishes that evidence that is not relevant is not admissible. Rule 702 provides that "if scientific, technical or other specialized knowledge will assist the trier of fact to understand the evidence or to determine a fact in issue, a witness qualified as an expert by knowledge, skill, experience, training, or education, may testify in the form of an opinion or otherwise."

Case

General Electric v. Joiner, 118 S.Ct. 512 (1997)

Issue
Expert witness testimony standard

Summary
Robert Joiner, a Georgia electrician and a chronic smoker, was diagnosed with small-cell lung cancer. He had been exposed to contaminated transformers during his work and claimed that the toxins had promoted his cancer. Regarding the expert testimony, the court had to determine which standard to use.

Holding
Expert testimony was decided to be inadmissible, because in this case it was an unsupported assertion.

Case

Kumho Tire Co. v. Carmichael, 119 S.Ct. 1167 (1999)

Issue
Expert witness testimony standard

Summary
Patrick Carmichael's rear tire blew out on his van, causing him to be involved in a fatal accident. The Carmichael family sued the tire's maker and distributor, claiming it was defective. The court had to decide whether or not to allow expert testimony from engineers and technicians regarding the car's tire.

Holding
The United States Supreme Court agreed that a trial judge may use the reliability factors discussed in Daubert, since engineering testimony is scientific. The Court held that the District Court had not abused its discretion in excluding the evidence. The expert witness could not reliably determine the cause of the tire's separation and had applied rules that others in his field did not use.

chapter ten

Civil

Americans with Disabilities Act (ADA)

Case

Carter v. General Motors, 361 Mich. 577, 106 N.W.2d 105 (1960)

Issue
Workers' compensation

Summary
James Carter, a machine operator who worked on assembly line production at General Motors, suffered from schizophrenia and a personality disorder. He wanted disability compensation, claiming that the stress of his job precipitated psychosis.

Holding
A compensable disability needs to be caused by a single physical injury or a single mental shock to the plaintiff. So long as the precipitant to the injury was work related, the court ruled, the injury is subject to compensation under the Workers' Compensation framework.

Case

School Board of Nassau County Florida v. Arline, 480 U.S. 273 (1987)

Issue
Employer discrimination and disability

Summary
Ms. Arline was fired from her teaching job due to a tuberculosis diagnosis. She argued that a contagious disease should be considered a physical impairment.

Holding
Contagious diseases are a physical impairment. This ruling laid the foundation for protection of HIV patients from discrimination at work.

Case

Pennsylvania Department of Corrections v. Yeskey, 188 S.Ct. 1952 (1998)

Issue
Prisoners and Americans with Disabilities Act (ADA)

Summary
Ronald Yeskey was sentenced to 18–36 months in a Pennsylvania correctional facility. He was recommended for placement in a motivational boot camp, the successful completion of which would make him eligible for early parole. Due to his hypertension, the program refused to admit him. He sued alleging that this was a violation of his rights under the ADA.

Holding
The statute states that any "public entity" cannot discriminate against any "qualified individual with a disability." Mr. Yeskey was a qualified individual and the Pennsylvania Department of Corrections is a public entity. Prison inmates are entitled to protection under the ADA.

Case

Bragdon v. Abbott, 118 S.Ct. 2198 (1998)

Issue
Qualification for disability

Summary
Sidney Abbott, infected with HIV but asymptomatic, went to her dentist for a cavity filling. Dr. Randon Bragdon agreed to do the filling but said it would need to be done in the hospital and Ms. Abbott would be responsible for costs. She declined the treatment and sued Dr. Bragdon for violating her rights under the ADA.

Holding
HIV infection does constitute a disability under the ADA.

Case

Olmstead v. L.C., 119 S.Ct. 2176 (1999)

Issue
Disability and the mentally retarded

Summary

L.C. and E.W. were mentally retarded women diagnosed with schizophrenia and personality disorder, respectively, and confined to the Georgia Regional Hospital psychiatric unit. Each woman stabilized and their doctors agreed that they were ready for community living. They remained hospitalized, however, because the state lacked sufficient resources to place them in a less restrictive environment. A suit was filed raising the issue of confinement as a matter of discrimination.

Holding

Placement in the community is in order when it is clinically appropriate. The ADA bans unjustified segregation of the disabled. In this case, the court held that unjustified institutional isolation discriminates in two ways:

- It perpetuates unwarranted assumptions and stigma
- It severely diminishes the everyday life activities of individuals including family involvement, socialization, working, economic independence, education, and cultural enrichment

Case

Sutton v. United Airlines, Inc., 119S.Ct. 2139 (1999)

Issue

Accommodations for disabilities

Summary

Two sisters both had myopia and applied to be pilots. They argued that myopia is a disability and that the airline must accommodate them.

Holding

Persons with disabilities must be accommodated.

Case

Toyota Motor Manufacturing Company v. Williams, 534 U.S. 184 (2002)

Issue

ADA standards

Summary

Ella Williams was an employee of a Toyota auto plant, where she developed bilateral carpal tunnel syndrome and could no longer work. She argued that work is a major life activity and therefore she should be covered by the ADA.

Holding

Working is a major life activity. The Americans with Disabilities Act Amendments Act (ADAAA) defined two lists of major life activities that qualify under ADA analysis:

- General acts (eating, sleeping, hearing, walking, working, etc.)
- Major bodily functions (immune system, cell growth, circulation, endocrine system, etc.)

Case

Hargrave v. Vermont, 340 F.3d 27 (2d Cir 2003)

Issue

ADA and power of attorney (POA)

Summary

Nancy Hargrave had schizophrenia and was hospitalized. Providers wanted to treat her with antipsychotic medication. She had previously completed a POA where she refused to ever accept electroconvulsive therapy or psychiatric medications. VT Law 114 allowed the petitioner (hospital) to force medication on Hargrave. She contested this arguing that it was discriminatory and did not uphold her POA.

Holding

The ADA prohibits discrimination against the mentally ill who refuse treatment via a POA.

Emotional harm

Case

Dillon v. Legg, 69 Cal. Rptr. 72, 441 P.2d 912 (1968)

Issue

Psychic injury

Summary

Erin Lee Dillon, crossing the street with her mother and sister, was killed by an automobile. There were two causes of action in this suit:

- For the sister's fear and distress for her own safety
- For the mother who suffered horror and fright as a result of witnessing the collision

Since Erin's sister could have also been killed by the car, she was considered to be within the "zone of danger." The children's mother, however, was further away and therefore not personally endangered by the collision.

Holding
Both causes of action held.

- The sister was in the "zone of danger" and was personally endangered by the defendant's automobile.
- California Supreme Court eviscerated the "zone of danger" distinction and held that the mother's fright and horror incurred by the collision must be considered and held in favor of the mother's action against the negligent defendant.

Insurance coverage

Case

Corcoran v. United Healthcare, Inc., 965 F.2d 1321, 1992

Issue
Medical insurance plans and Employee Retirement Income Security Act (ERISA)

Summary
Florence Corcoran received medical care for her pregnancy through the Bell Plan, administered by Blue Cross and Blue Shield. Her plan required that participants obtain advance approval for certain medical procedures via a third party, United Healthcare (UHC). Corcoran's pregnancy was difficult and her doctor ordered her to be hospitalized but the insurance carrier, UHC, refused. They would only cover ten hours a day of home nursing care and not hospitalization. After the fetus went into distress and died, Corcoran filed a lawsuit for wrongful death against Blue Cross and United.

Holding
According to the Fifth Circuit, the federal ERISA of 1974 preempted a malpractice action in state court against a company providing precertification review of medical services.

Case

Dukes v. U.S. Healthcare, Inc., 57 F.3d 350 (3rd Cir. 1995)

Issue
Health maintenance organization (HMO) and negligence

Summary

Darryl Dukes received medical care through an HMO organized by U.S. Healthcare. Dukes' primary care physician gave him a prescription order for a blood test, but the lab refused to draw his blood. Eventually he got the blood test, after it was arranged by another physician. The tests showed an extremely high blood sugar level, and shortly thereafter, Dukes died. His wife, Cecilia Dukes, brought suit alleging negligence of the facilities and physicians involved. She argued that Dukes' condition could have been diagnosed and treated through a timely blood test. She also sued the HMO under "agency theory" for failing to provide expected care and for failing to exercise reasonable care in the selection and monitoring of its personnel.

Holding

The Third Circuit held that the federal Employee Retirement Income Security Act (ERISA) does not preempt actions in state court against HMOs for negligence in the quality of service provided.

Case

Aetna v. McCabe, 556 F.Supp. 1342 (1983)

Issue

Malpractice insurance coverage

Summary

Gale Greenberg saw Dr. Donald McCabe for treatment of anxiety in 1968. The doctor administered an illicit drug during therapy and then Greenberg began having sexual relations with McCabe. In the midst of an altercation, Greenberg fell and sustained a fracture to her skull. She brought suit against McCabe alleging his negligent care and treatment had caused her injury. Aetna Life and Casualty Company, McCabe's malpractice carrier, provided an attorney to represent him. The jury concluded in favor of Greenberg and awarded her over $500,000, but Aetna refused to pay, arguing that McCabe's sexual involvement with Greenberg did not constitute a professional service and that he was therefore not entitled to insurance coverage.

Holding

Pennsylvania District Court concluded that an insurance carrier must pay all but punitive damages for a physician who engaged in a sexual relationship with his patient, after a jury had concluded that this was medical malpractice.

Sexual harassment

Case

Meritor Savings Bank v. Vinson, 477 U.S. 57 (1986)

Issue
Sexual harassment and Civil Rights Act

Summary
Michelle Vinson was hired as a teller-trainee at Meritor Savings and quickly rose through the ranks. She became an assistant branch manager and took an indefinite sick leave after which she was fired for excessive use of her sick leave. Vinson filed a Title VII suit against Meritor Savings Bank, alleging that it was liable for sexual harassment perpetrated by its employee and vice president, Mr. Sidney Taylor. Vinson claimed there had been forty to fifty sexual encounters over the span of four years ranging from fondling to indecent exposure to rape. Vinson asserted that she never reported these events for fear of losing her job.

Holding
This was the first United States Supreme Court case to address sexual harassment as cause of action. The Court looked to the position taken by the Equal Employment Opportunity Commission (EEOC). Hostile claims are actionable under Title VII (which affords employees the right to work in an environment free from discriminatory intimidation, ridicule, and insult), but the conduct must be severe. Vinson was in a hostile environment. The test was not whether her participation was "voluntary," but rather whether Mr. Taylor's advances were unwelcome.

Case

Harris v. Forklift Systems, Inc., 114 S.Ct. 367 (1993)

Issue
Sexual harassment in the workplace

Summary
Teresa Harris was a manager at Forklift Systems, Inc., where Charles Hardy was the president. Throughout her employment, Mr. Hardy frequently directed offensive remarks at Ms. Harris, often in the presence of other employees. Comments were sexual and discriminatory gender statements. Harris sued under Title VII and initially the District Court found

that although Hardy's comments were offensive, they were not severe enough to be expected to seriously affect Harris' psychological well-being.

Holding
The Court agreed with Harris and established the Reasonable Person Test. This was a Civil Rights issue, and therefore, evidence of harm or damage is not needed.

Case

Oncale v. Sundowner Offshore Services, Inc., 118 S.Ct. 998 (1998)

Issue
Same-sex sexual harassment

Summary
Joseph Oncale was a roustabout on an eight-man crew on an oil platform in the Gulf of Mexico, where he was forcibly subjected to sexual abuse by coworkers and threatened with rape. He sued but the United States District Court of the Eastern District of Louisiana dismissed the case holding there was no cause of action for same-sex sexual harassment.

Holding
When Congress enacted Title VII it wanted to prohibit discrimination based on sex. Title VII, therefore, bans an objective level of abuse as a condition of employment.

Sex

Case

Roy v. Hartogs, 381 N.Y.S. 2d 587 (1976)

Issue
Sex with patients

Summary
Julie Roy received psychotherapy from Dr. Hartogs, which included sexual intercourse as part of therapy. She sued Hartogs, arguing that his improper treatment emotionally and mentally injured her to such an extent that she was required to seek hospitalization twice.

Holding
Sexual intercourse with his patient constituted medical malpractice.

chapter eleven

Criminal

Criminal competency

Case

Dusky v. U.S., 362 U.S. 402, 80 S.Ct. 788 (1960)

Issue
Test for competency to stand trial

Summary
Milton Dusky was convicted of kidnapping and the interstate transport of a minor. A question of his competency to stand trial arose when reports noted that he was not able to discern reality from unreality and he showed signs of confused and suspicious thinking. The trial court, nevertheless, ruled that Dusky had sufficient mental capacity to stand trial, citing the fact that he was oriented. Defense argued that confirmation of orientation was not a fair assessment of his competence.

Holding
The United States Supreme Court overturned Dusky's conviction. The competency standard has become known as the Dusky Standard: "The test must be whether [the defendant] has sufficient present ability to consult with his lawyer with a reasonable degree of rational understanding—and whether he has a rational as well as a factual understanding of the proceedings against him."

Case

Wilson v. U.S., 129 U.S. App. D.C. 107, 391 F.2d 460 (1968)

Issue
Amnesia and competency to stand trial

Summary
Robert Wilson was charged with five counts of assault and robbery in Washington, D.C. After the crime spree, he engaged in a high-speed car chase that led to an accident from which he suffered a head injury resulting

in retrograde amnesia. Wilson had no memory of the events he was charged with and his defense argued that he was incompetent to stand trial because amnesia precluded him from assisting his attorney in the defense.

Holding

Amnesia does not per se equate incompetence to stand trial. The trial court found Wilson to be competent, pointing out that he had the capacity to understand the details of the case by relying on other sources of information, he could follow the proceedings in court, and he could discuss the case with his attorney in a rational way. Memory loss would bar prosecution of a criminal case only when the defendant's memory was "crucial" to the presentation of a defense.

Case

Sieiling v. Eyman, 478 F.2d 211 (9th Cir. Ariz. 1973)

Issue
Competence and pleading guilty

Summary
Gilbert Sieling, a psychotic man, was charged by the State of Arizona with multiple counts of assault. Sieling pled guilty and was convicted. Later, he appealed his conviction, contending that his plea should not have been accepted because he was mentally incompetent to make it.

Holding
The defendant's competence in this situation must be measured by a higher standard, given that entering a guilty plea was a very serious decision with substantial consequences.

Case

Godinez v. Moran, 61 U.S.L.W. 4749, 113 S.Ct. 2680 (1993)

Issue
Competence and pleading guilty

Summary
Richard Moran was arrested after a crime spree in which he killed three people and then shot himself in a suicide attempt. He was found competent to stand trial and the court accepted his guilty plea and sentenced Moran to death for three murders. Moran filed a claim that he had been mentally incompetent to represent himself and enter the guilty plea.

Holding

United States Supreme Court reaffirmed Moran's conviction stating that there could only be one standard for competence in criminal cases. If one is competent to stand trial, then he or she must be competent to plead guilty.

Case

Cooper v. Oklahoma, 116 S.Ct. 1923 (1996)

Issue

Competency standard

Summary

Bryan Cooper was convicted of murdering an 86-year-old man in a burglary and was sentenced to death. Despite displaying bizarre behavior where he talked about spirits and the belief that his attorney might kill him, Cooper was declared competent by the court because Oklahoma's statute required a finding otherwise by clear and convincing evidence. The defense argued that the clear and convincing standard of proof violated the due process clause of the Fourteenth Amendment.

Holding

Oklahoma law did violate due process. In effect, the law allowed the state to try a defendant who was more likely than not to be incompetent. The new standard became preponderance of the evidence.

Case

Indiana v. Edwards, 554 U.S. 164 (2008)

Issue

Competency to represent oneself

Summary

Ahmed Edwards was charged with attempted murder after he shot at a security guard while trying to steal shoes. He appeared mentally ill but wanted to proceed pro se with his defense.

Holding

When a defendant appears to be severely mentally ill, the state must stop him or her from representing him- or herself.

Insanity

Case

M'Naghten's Case, 8 Eng. Rep. 718, 8 Eng. Rep. 722 (1843)

Issue
Insanity test

Summary
Daniel M'Naghten suffered from paranoid psychosis, in which he believed that he was being persecuted by the Tory party. In 1843 he shot and killed Edward Drummond, the secretary to Prime Minister Robert Peel. The defense portrayed M'Naghten as an insane person who had been in a state of terror. After hearing expert testimony, the jury acquitted M'Naghten on the grounds of insanity.

Holding
M'Naghten's Rule: For a defendant to be found insane, "It must be clearly provided that, at the time of the committing of the act, the party accused was laboring under such a defect of reason, from disease of the mind, as not to know the nature and quality of the act he was doing; or, if he did know it, that he did not know he was doing what was wrong."

Case

Durham v. U.S., 94 U.S. App. D.C. 228, 214 F.2d 862 (1954)

Issue
Insanity test redefined

Summary
Monte Durham was charged for housebreaking. He had a long history of psychiatric illness including personality disorder and antisocial behavior. He raised an insanity defense.

Holding
Judge David Bazelon and the U.S. Court of Appeals for the District of Columbia Circuit redefined the test for insanity in a criminal case. A defendant was "not criminally responsible if his unlawful act was the product of a mental disease or defect."

Case

Washington v. U.S., 129 U.S. App. D.C. 29, 390 F.2d 444 (1967)

Issue

Insanity and psychiatric expert testimony

Summary

Mr. Washington was convicted of rape, robbery, and assault. He had pre-sented an insanity defense where lawyers and expert witnesses relied heavily on medical jargon during the trial.

Holding

Washington's conviction was upheld. Judge Bazelon offered suggestions for how psychiatric experts should testify, emphasizing that they should with-hold the use of jargon that could hinder juries in reaching their decisions.

Case

Frendak v. U.S., 408 A.2d 364 (D.C. 1979)

Issue

Imposition of insanity defense

Summary

Paula Frendak murdered her coworker and although she was competent to stand trial, the court found her to appear psychotic and tried to impose the insanity defense.

Holding

A trial judge cannot force the insanity defense on a defendant. The court must defer to the defendant's decision about the insanity defense as long as it was made intelligently and voluntarily.

Case

Ake v. Oklahoma, 470 U.S. 68, 105 S.Ct. 1087 (1985)

Issue

Preparation of insanity defense

Summary

Glen Burton Ake was arrested for murder but due to bizarre behavior and delusions, the court committed him to a state hospital for examination of competence to stand trial. He was found competent after treatment with Thorazine and then presented an insanity defense. There was no expert testimony regarding Ake's mental state at the time of the offense, and the jury convicted Ake and sentenced him to death. Ake argued that he should have had access to a psychiatrist's help in forming his insanity defense.

Holding
When an indigent defendant shows that his sanity is likely to be a significant issue, the Fourteenth Amendment does require the state to provide access to psychiatric services.

Case

Foucha v. Louisiana, 112 S.Ct. 1780 (1992)

Issue
Commitment of persons adjudicated Not Guilty by Reason of Insanity (NGRI)

Summary
Foucha was convicted of burglary and illegal discharge of a firearm. He was found NGRI and was committed for treatment. The superintendent of the hospital ultimately diagnosed Foucha with drug-induced psychosis, reported that he had recovered, and recommended that he be released. Foucha complained that those adjudicated NGRI were being held in state hospitals longer than necessary.

Holding
A defendant found NGRI could only be committed to a psychiatric hospital as long as he continued to be both mentally ill and dangerous. It might be acceptable to confine an NGRI acquittee if the nature and duration of the confinement had a medical justification and were tailored to a specific safety concern.

The Supreme Court relied on three prior decisions to reach its conclusion: *Addington v. Texas, Jones v. U.S.,* and *Vitek v. Jones.*

Testimony

Case

State v. Hurd, 173 N.J. Super. 333, 414 A.2d 291 (1980)

Issue
Hypnotically refreshed memories

Summary
Paul Hurd, the defendant in an assault case, filed a motion in a New Jersey superior court to suppress the victim's identification of him in court. Jane

Bell, the accuser, had no recollection of her attacker and only identified Hurd after hypnosis.

Holding

The court granted the defendant's motion to suppress the identification as a matter of due process. Expert testimony by Dr. Orne indicated that hypnotic recall is often unreliable and that a hypnotized subject is highly vulnerable to suggestion, is likely to have diminished critical judgment, and may fill in gaps in memory by confabulation when pressed to give an answer.

Dr. Orne established a list of safeguards to hypnosis:

- Licensed psychiatrists trained in a hospital could be qualified as hypnotists.
- Hypnotists should be independent and not hired by the prosecution or defense.
- All details obtained by the hypnotist should be written.
- Sessions should be video-recorded.
- Only the therapist and subject should be present during hypnosis (i.e., no lawyers).

Case

People v. Shirley, 181 Cal. Rptr. 243 (1982)

Issue

Hypnosis and reliability

Summary

Catherine C. was the complaining witness in a rape trial. She was a bar maid who testified that the defendant had threatened her with weapons and raped her. Prior to the trial, the prosecutor had Catherine C. hypnotized, but at trial she was inconsistent, dramatic, and self-contradicted many times. The jury still convicted the defendant of rape. The defense argued that hypnotically refreshed memories should be excluded during testimony.

Holding

California Supreme Court overturned the conviction and ruled that it was an error to allow Catherine C. to testify after having undergone hypnosis. The Court found a widespread consensus that hypnotically enhanced testimony is not reliable.

Case

Rock v. Arkansas, 483 U.S. 44, 107 S.Ct. 2704 (1987)

Issue
Hypnotically refreshed memories

Summary
Vickie Rock fought with her husband and shot him. When police arrived, she told them there was a domestic dispute where she had felt threatened. Rock was not allowed to introduce hypnotically refreshed memories from which she had learned that the pistol misfired and the shooting was therefore an accident. She was convicted of manslaughter and appealed her conviction. She argued that the State of Arkansas, in excluding her own hypnotically refreshed testimony from trial, had infringed on her constitutional right to testify on her own behalf.

Holding
This was a violation of the defendant's rights under the Fifth, Sixth, and Fourteenth Amendments. Essentially, hypnosis testimony is allowed if the defendant can use it for exoneration.

Diminished capacity

Case

People v. Patterson, 39 N.Y.2d 288, 347 N.E.2d 898 (1976)

Issue
Burden of proof and emotional duress

Summary
Gordon Patterson killed a man whom he found in bed with his estranged wife. The burden of proof was placed on Patterson to show that he acted under extreme emotional duress. Patterson argued that this violated his due process.

Holding
The court reasoned that extreme emotional disturbance does not contradict intent but rather serves to explain the defendant's intentional action.

Case

Ibn-Tamas v. U.S., 407 A.2d 626 (1979)

Issue
Expert testimony and battered wife syndrome

Summary
Beverly Ibn-Tamas was convicted of the murder of her husband in the Superior Court of the District of Columbia. The defense alleged that her husband, a physician, was a violent man who had assaulted her on numerous occasions and that she was in imminent danger due to his repeated threats and violence. The defense offered the testimony of a psychologist on the subject of the battered wife syndrome.

Holding
Expert testimony on battered wife syndrome was not, in principle, inadmissible. The court held that the expert testimony here was beyond the ordinary knowledge of the jury, so that its value did outweigh any prejudicial effect.

Case

Montana v. Egelhoff, 116 S.Ct. 2013 (1996)

Issue
Voluntary intoxication and culpability

Summary
James Egelhoff spent a night drinking heavily and was accused of shooting and killing two acquaintances while intoxicated. His defense was that his extreme intoxication rendered him mentally incapable of committing murder. The main question in this case was whether the court should consider his intoxication.

Holding
The United States Supreme Court held that due process does not guarantee to the defendant the right to present all relevant evidence.

Criminal procedure

Case

North Carolina v. Alford, 400 U.S. 25, 91 S.Ct. 160 (1970)

Issue
Entering into a plea bargain

Summary
Alford was charged with first-degree murder, and following his attorney's advice, he entered into a plea bargain where he pled guilty to

second-degree murder, all the while contesting he was really inno-
cent. After thirty years in prison, Alford sought postconviction release
stating that he only pled guilty because he was afraid of the death
penalty.

Holding
The offender's Fifth Amendment right against self-incrimination was
not violated because his plea was entered into knowingly, intelligently,
and voluntarily.

Case

Colorado v. Connelly, 479 U.S. 157, 107 S.Ct. 515 (1986)

Issue
Voluntary confessions

Summary
Connelly, suffering from auditory hallucinations and a serious mental disorder, had approached a Denver police officer and spontaneously
reported that he had committed a murder. The officer immediately
advised Connelly of his rights (under *Miranda v. Arizona*, 384 U.S. 436,
1966). Connelly said that he understood and wanted to talk because his
conscience bothered him. Connelly was charged with the murder and
later contested that his confession was based on hallucinatory commands
and therefore not voluntary.

Holding
The United States Supreme Court reversed Colorado's Supreme Court
decision. The United States Supreme Court held that the admissibility of a confession is governed by state rules of evidence rather than
Miranda or other decisions involving police misconduct. Writing for the
majority, Chief Justice Rehnquist found that there had been no demon-
stration of police misconduct and therefore no violation of the defendant's right to due process.

Case

Miranda v. Arizona, 384 U.S. 436 (1966)

Issue
Miranda rights

Summary
Ernesto Miranda was arrested by the Phoenix Police Department based on circumstantial evidence linking him to the kidnapping and rape of a 15-year-old girl. After two hours of interrogation by police officers, Miranda signed a confession to the rape charge. He was not advised of his right to remain silent, nor was he informed that his statements during the interrogation would be used against him. At trial, when prosecutors offered Miranda's written confession as evidence, his court-appointed lawyer, Alvin Moore, objected, arguing that the confession was not truly voluntary and should be excluded.

Holding
Due to the coercive nature of the custodial interrogation by police, no confession could be admissible under the Fifth Amendment self-incrimination clause and the Sixth Amendment right to an attorney unless a suspect had been made aware of his rights and the suspect had then waived them.

Case

Robinson v. California, 370 U.S. 660, 82 S.Ct. 1417 (1962)

Issue
Status crimes

Summary
Mr. Robinson was stopped by police who noticed track marks on his arms from intravenous drug use. He was arrested and convicted of being a drug addict. In California in the 1960s, it was a misdemeanor to be addicted to narcotics. Robinson argued this was cruel and unusual punishment and violated his rights under the Eighth and Fourteenth Amendments.

Holding
Addiction is an illness, analogous to mental illness or leprosy. It would universally be considered cruel to punish people for such illnesses. This case helped remove other status crimes (e.g., homelessness, vagrancy).

Case

Powell v. Texas, 392 U.S. 514, 88 S.Ct. 2145 (1968)

Issue
Public intoxication

Summary

Powell was convicted of public intoxication. He was a chronic alcoholic and argued that drinking was a compulsion and not a choice, so arrest for such a disease was equivalent to cruel and unusual punishment.

Holding

Powell was convicted not for the status of being an alcoholic but rather for public intoxication, which was a crime.

chapter twelve

Death penalty

Death penalty

Case

Estelle v. Smith, 451 U.S. 454, 101 S.Ct. 1866 (1981)

Issue
Psychiatric testimony at criminal sentencing

Summary
Dr. James Grigson evaluated Ernest Smith, charged with the murder of a store clerk in a robbery, for competency to stand trial. After being found competent and later convicted of the crime, Smith had another sentencing hearing per Texas law. Dr. Grigson was called as a surprise witness to testify about Smith's risk of future dangerousness, although he had never evaluated him for this matter. Dr. Grigson referred to Smith during testimony as a psychopath and believed that he was a high risk for future criminal acts. Smith claimed Grigson's testimony violated his Fifth and Sixth Amendment rights.

Holding
There was a violation of Smith's Fifth Amendment right against self-incrimination and also of his Sixth Amendment right to have counsel.

Case

Barefoot v. Estelle, 463 U.S. 880, 103 S.Ct. 3383 (1983)

Issue
Death penalty and hypothetical testimony

Summary
Thomas Barefoot was convicted of the murder of a police officer in Texas. At his sentencing hearing there was a question about Barefoot's probability of committing further violent criminal acts. The prosecution called Dr. James Grigson, who had never examined Barefoot, and asked him to answer hypothetical questions.

Holding

The United States Supreme Court would not bar psychiatrists from predicting future violence. Hypothetical testimony without examination was permitted.

Case

Ford v. Wainwright, 477 U.S. 399, 106 S.Ct. 2595 (1986)

Issue

Competency to be executed

Summary

Alvin Ford was convicted of murder in Florida and was sentenced to die. He showed signs of psychosis and even believed that he had won a landmark case against his state and would not be executed. Since Florida law prohibited the execution of an insane person, the state appointed three psychiatrists who evaluated Ford together for a total of thirty minutes after which they found him competent. Ford's counsel filed a writ of habeas corpus and asked the court to consider whether the Eighth Amendment barred the execution of an insane person and whether Florida's procedure satisfied the requirements of due process.

Holding

The Eighth Amendment did bar the execution of the insane. Florida's procedure did not give Ford a fair hearing.

Case

Thompson v. Oklahoma, 487 U.S. 815 (1988)

Issue

Death penalty and juveniles

Summary

William Wayne Thompson, a 15-year-old at the time of his crime, was tried as an adult for murder, found guilty, and sentenced to death. He objected on the argument that his Eighth and Fourteenth Amendment rights were violated.

Holding

It is not constitutional to execute a minor. As society matured, the standards of decency had also evolved.

Case

Stanford v. Kentucky, 492 U.S. 361 (1989)

Issue
Death penalty and juveniles

Summary
Kevin Stanford, 17 years old, raped and murdered a gas station atten-
dant in Jefferson County, Kentucky. He was convicted and sentenced
to death. One year earlier, the case of *Thompson v. Oklahoma* had determined that it was a violation of the Eighth and Fourteenth Amendments
to execute a minor.

Holding
The Governor of Kentucky supported the death penalty for Stanford, who
was executed.

Case

Penry v. Lynaugh, 57 U.S.L.M. 4958 (1989)

Issue
Mitigating factors and execution

Summary
Penry, who had mental retardation and an IQ of 50–63, was charged and
convicted for the rape and murder of a woman in Texas. The defense
argued that a judge's failure to instruct a jury about mitigating psychological evidence constituted a violation of the Eighth Amendment. The
defense also argued that the Eighth Amendment prohibited the execution
of the mentally retarded absolutely.

Holding
Penry's retardation, which rendered him with the mental and social age
of a child, was relevant. When mitigating evidence has been presented,
the jury must be given instructions to consider such. The Court declined
to prohibit the execution of the retarded under all circumstances. Justice
O'Connor commented on the "evolving standard of decency," but there
was not yet a national consensus on the execution of the retarded.

Case

Payne v. Tennessee, 111 S.Ct. 2597 (1991)

Issue
Victim impact statements

Summary

Pervis Payne was convicted of the brutal murder of a mother and her 2-year-old daughter. Three-year-old Nicholas was also stabbed by Payne, but he survived. The jury found Payne guilty. During sentencing the prosecution presented Nicholas's grandmother, who testified about the severe impact of the crime on the small boy who knew that his mother and sister had been killed. After hearing this, the jury sentenced Payne to death. Payne argued that the admittance of the victim impact statement had been a constitutional violation.

Holding

The United States Supreme Court overturned its previous decision on this matter and allowed the victim impact statement. The Court said "stare decisis is not an inexorable command." Allowing the statement was not a violation of the Eighth Amendment as Payne argued.

Case

State v. Perry, 610 So.2d 746 (La. 1992)

Issue

Competency to be executed and forced medications

Summary

Michael Perry, a man with schizophrenia, was convicted of murdering his mother, father, nephew, and two cousins and was sentenced to death. During his evaluation for competency to be executed, experts reported that he was incurable but psychotic symptoms would lessen if he took antipsychotic medication. This would render him competent for execution.

Holding

Louisiana Supreme Court held that forcibly medicating Perry for competence to be executed violated his right to privacy and amounted to cruel and unusual punishment.

Case

Atkins v. Virginia, 122 S.Ct. 2242 (2002)

Issue

Death penalty and the mentally retarded

Summary

Daryl Atkins was a mentally retarded man with an IQ of 59 who was convicted of abduction, armed robbery, and capital murder in the state of

Virginia. He was sentenced to death. Atkins argued that it was a violation of the Eighth Amendment to sentence a mentally retarded person to execution.

Holding

The execution of the mentally retarded is equal to cruel and unusual punishment and does violate the Eighth Amendment. This decision was largely based on polling data that showed Americans were not in support of the execution of the mentally retarded.

Case

Roper v. Simmons, 543 U.S. 551 (2005)

Issue

Death penalty and juveniles

Summary

Christopher Simmons, 17 years old, brutally raped and murdered Shirley Cook. The State of Missouri sought to execute Simmons and he was sentenced to death. Based on evolving standards of decency in the nation, the execution of a minor, similar to that of a mentally retarded individual, was a violation of the Eighth and Fourteenth Amendments.

Holding

The United States Supreme Court opined that execution of a minor does violate the Eighth and Fourteenth Amendments.

chapter thirteen

Corrections/correctional healthcare

Prisoners' rights

Case

Estelle v. Gamble, 429 U.S. 97, 97 S.Ct. 285 (1976)

Issue
Prisoner's right to treatment

Summary
Gamble filed a Section 1983, claiming that as a prisoner he had received inadequate medical treatment. He argued this violated his Eighth Amendment right.

Holding
The prisoner's medical care qualified as deliberate indifference.

Case

Washington v. Harper, 494 U.S. 210, 110 S.Ct. 1028 (1990)

Issue
Prisoners and medication refusal

Summary
Walter Harper was sentenced to the Washington State Penitentiary in 1976 for robbery. He was treated with antipsychotics and was eventually released on parole. Parole was revoked when he assaulted two nurses at the Harborview Medical Center in Seattle. Upon reincarceration, he was sent to a psychiatric hospital within the Department of Corrections. Harper refused medication, and he filed suit under 42 U.S.C., Section 1983, claiming that the State had violated the due process, equal protection, and free speech clauses of the Constitution.

Holding

The United States Supreme Court granted certiorari. Harper possessed a liberty interest in refusing antipsychotic medication under the due process clause of the Fourteenth Amendment as well as under the state law. Under the due process clause, however, this liberty interest must be balanced against the prisoner's medical interests and the State's legitimate interest in prison safety and security.

Case

Riggins v. Nevada, 504 U.S. 127 (1992)

Issue

Forced medication and fair trial

Summary

David Riggins was arrested and charged with murder in Nevada. During his pretrial detention, Riggins was involuntarily given an antipsychotic medication, Mellaril, to treat auditory hallucinations, during which time he gained the competency to stand trial. He pled insanity and his attorney asked for the suspension of medication because it would affect Riggins's demeanor and mental state at trial, and the jury would not see his true mental condition. Riggins was forcibly medicated throughout the trial and was convicted of murder.

Holding

The Fourteenth Amendment must provide at least as much protection for a pretrial defendant as it does for a convicted prison inmate. Involuntary medication of a pretrial detainee violates both the Sixth and Fourteenth Amendments if the State does not establish a need for the treatment.

Case

Farmer v. Brennan, 114 S.Ct. 1970 (1994)

Issue

Deliberate indifference

Summary

Dee Farmer was a transsexual who appeared female after having undergone hormone therapy and breast implantation. He was imprisoned and housed in the general population where he was beaten and raped by a cellmate. Farmer filed suit in federal court, alleging that his Eighth Amendment right had been violated when prison officials placed him in the general population.

Holding

In this case the mens rea for deliberate indifference was subjective recklessness, because the risk was so obvious that the prison official surely
knew yet ignored it.

Case

Sell v. U.S., 539 U.S. 166 (2003)

Issue

Forced medication for competency

Summary

Dr. Sell was a dentist who was accused of Medicaid fraud and convicted.
He was found incompetent to stand trial and was sent to a psychiatric
hospital where doctors wanted to forcibly medicate him to restore Sell's
competence to stand trial.

Holding

Involuntary treatment to restore competence to stand trial is allowed if
the accused meet these criteria:

- Medication is appropriate
- Treatment does not likely undermine the trial's fairness
- Medication is the least intrusive alternative
- Treatment furthers a government trial-related interest

Case

Coleman v. Wilson, 912 F.Supp. 1282 (1995)

Issue

A prisoner's right to treatment/medical care

Summary

Prisoners with psychiatric disorders filed a Section 1983 suit. They argued
that mental healthcare by the California Department of Corrections was
inadequate and violated their Eighth and Fourteenth Amendment rights.

Holding

In a blockbuster decision, the court found these critical findings in the prison:

- Inadequate screening
- Chronic understaffing

- Incompetent staff
- Problems with medication management
- Inappropriate punishments for patients with mental illness
- Deficient medical records
- Understaffing
- Deliberate indifference

chapter fourteen

Legal systems/basic law

Civil commitment

Case

Baxstrom v. Herold, 383 U.S. 107, 86 S.Ct. 760 (1966)

Issue
Prisoners and due process

Summary
Johnnie Baxstrom, convicted of assault, was committed to a New York prison. The prison authorized his transfer to Dannemora State Hospital, a psychiatric hospital for prisoners, after he was found insane. When Baxstrom's penal sentence was about to end, the hospital director applied for civil commitment. This was based on the opinion of two hospital physicians that Baxstrom was still mentally ill and in need of hospital care. Baxstrom filed a writ of habeas corpus.

Holding
New York's statute for civil commitment of a prisoner at the expiration of a penal sentence violated the equal protection clause of the Fourteenth Amendment in two respects:

- All nonprisoners facing civil commitment have the right to a full jury trial to determine whether they are mentally ill.
- No other person may be committed to a Department of Corrections facility without a judicial finding.

Case

Lake v. Cameron, 124 U.S. App. D.C. 264, 364 F.2d 657 (1966)

Issue
Least restrictive setting

Summary
Catherine Lake, an elderly senile "bag lady," was civilly committed to St. Elizabeth's Hospital. She contested her detention as it was highly restrictive.

Holding
Judge Bazelon held that a person should be in the least restrictive alternative for treatment.

Case

Jackson v. Indiana, 406 U.S. 715, 92 S.Ct. 1845 (1972)

Issue
Incompetency and commitment. A person found incompetent to stand trial but not yet convicted may only be committed for a period of time long enough to restore competence or to determine whether he or she will become competent in the foreseeable future.

Summary
Theon Jackson, a deaf and mute man, stole $9.00 in property and cash. Trial court found him incompetent to stand trial and committed him to the Indiana Department of Mental Health. Jackson's attorney filed a motion for a new trial arguing that his client would never become competent to stand trial and it was cruel to keep him locked up forever.

Holding
Indiana's indefinite commitment of a person as incompetent to stand trial violated both the equal protection and due process clauses of the Fourteenth Amendment. Due process requires that the nature and duration of confinement similarly relate to the purpose of commitment.

Case

Lessard v. Schmidt, 349 F. Supp. 1078 (E.D. Wis. 1972)

Issue
Due process and involuntary commitment

Summary
Alberta Lessard was picked up in front of her house by two police officers, who took her to the Mental Health Center in Milwaukee, Wisconsin. The Mental Health Center then requested that she become permanently committed although she was not informed of any of the proceedings. Lessard

retained an attorney who filed a class action in Federal District Court under 42 U.S.C. Section 1983 arguing that Wisconsin's involuntary commitment statute deprived her of due process rights.

Holding

Procedural safeguards are constitutionally required for commitment of the mentally ill:

- The patient must be given timely notice of charges and notice of all rights.
- A probable cause hearing must be held within forty-eight hours.
- The patient has the right to representation by an attorney.
- Hearsay evidence may not be admitted in the hearing.
- The patient retains the privilege against self-incrimination and must be informed that any information provided during examination may be used against him or her in the hearing.
- The State must prove beyond a reasonable doubt that the patient is both mentally ill and dangerous.
- The State must demonstrate that less restrictive alternatives to commitment are not available or not suitable.

Case

O'Connor v. Donaldson, 422 U.S. 563, 95 S.Ct. 2486 (1975)

Issue

Custodial care

Summary

Kenneth Donaldson, a man with schizophrenia, was committed to the Florida State Hospital. Donaldson repeatedly asked for discharge during his lengthy hospital stay, where he claimed he was not dangerous or mentally ill. He also claimed that he wasn't receiving any treatment. Superintendent O'Connor refused but almost immediately after O'Connor's retirement, Donaldson was released. Donaldson alleged that O'Connor had intentionally and maliciously deprived him of his constitutional right to liberty even though state law authorized indefinite custodial confinement of the mentally ill.

Holding

The United States Supreme Court held that a state cannot constitutionally confine a nondangerous person who can live safely in freedom by himself, or with the help of willing and responsible family members or friends. This case hastened the deinstitutionalization movement and many patients were released.

Case

Addington v. Texas, 441 U.S. 418, 99 S.Ct. 1804 (1979)

Issue
Civil commitment standard

Summary
Frank Addington's mother petitioned the Texas trial court to commit her son to a mental hospital. The standard for commitment at that time was "beyond a reasonable doubt."

Holding
The standard of proof for civil commitment was reduced to "clear and convincing evidence."

Case

Parham v. J.R. and J.L., 442 U.S. 584, 99 S.Ct. 2493 (1979)

Issue
Juvenile rights and psychiatric commitment

Summary
J.R. was one of two plaintiffs in a class-action suit brought in federal court by all minors detained for psychiatric treatment in Georgia. They were admitted to the hospital on a voluntary basis by their parents due to uncontrollable disruptive behaviors. The plaintiffs argued that Georgia's procedure for the voluntary commitment of minors was not constitutional.

Holding
The United States Supreme Court held that Georgia's procedure for the voluntary commitment of minors was constitutional. The Court held that parental authority could admit children to a psychiatric unit with safeguards:

- A psychiatric opinion that commitment is necessary
- A periodic review

Case

Vitek v. Jones, 445 U.S. 480, 100 S.Ct. 1254 (1980)

Issue

Transfer of prisoners and due process

Summary

Larry Jones, imprisoned for robbery, was sent to solitary confinement where he set a mattress on fire and suffered severe burns. He was transferred to the state mental hospital and challenged this transfer as a violation of procedural due process under the Fourteenth Amendment.

Holding

The United States Supreme Court agreed that Jones possessed a liberty interest in avoiding transfer to a mental hospital. Proper procedures for such a transfer would include:

- Written notice
- Adversarial hearing with an opportunity to present testimony and cross-examine witnesses
- An independent decision-maker
- Notice of rights and availability of legal counsel
- Independent legal assistance

Case

Jones v. U.S., 463 U.S. 354, 103 S.Ct. 3043 (1983)

Issue

Indefinite commitment

Summary

Michael Jones was arrested for attempting to steal a jacket from a department store. Appearing psychotic, Jones was sent to a psychiatric hospital where he was found competent to stand trial and entered an insanity plea. Still appearing ill at his hearing, the Court ordered a recommitment to the psychiatric hospital. After more than one year in the hospital, Jones petitioned the Court for unconditional release or a recommitment pursuant to civil commitment standards. This would entail a jury trial and proof by clear and convincing evidence that he was currently mentally ill and dangerous.

Holding

The purpose of commitment is treatment, not punishment. There is no correlation between the severity of offense for which a defendant was charged and the length of time necessary to recover from mental illness.

Case

Zinermon v. Burch, 494 U.S. 113, 110 S.Ct. 975 (1990)

Issue
Deprivation of liberty

Summary
Darrell Burch was taken to a psychiatric hospital after he was found wandering around a highway confused and hallucinating. At the hospital, he signed forms giving consent to admission and treatment on a psychiatric unit. He was transferred to a state hospital and signed additional forms for voluntary commitment and treatment, but progress notes indicated that he could not state the reason for his hospitalization, which went on for five months. Burch argued that he had been involuntarily hospitalized without legally adequate consent, thus depriving him of his liberty without due process in violation of the Fourteenth Amendment.

Holding
State employees admitted Burch as voluntary without determining whether he was mentally competent to sign the voluntary admission forms.

Right to die

Case

Cruzan v. Director, Missouri DMH, 497 U.S. 261, 110 S.Ct. 2841 (1990)

Issue
Right to refuse life-sustaining treatment

Summary
Nancy Cruzan entered into a "persistent vegetative state" after a car crash necessitating gastric tube feeding and hydration to keep her alive. After several years, when it became clear that she had no chance of regaining her mental faculties, her parents asked that her artificial nutrition be terminated. The hospital refused to honor this request without a court approval. Missouri courts had the right to require clear and convincing evidence about an individual's wishes.

Holding
The State's procedural requirement upheld the Constitution. Evidence of the incompetent's wishes as to the withdrawal of treatment needed to be proved by clear and convincing evidence.

Case

Washington v. Glucksberg, 117 S.Ct. 2258 (1997)

Issue
Physician-assisted suicide and due process

Summary
Physicians and patients joined by the nonprofit organization Compassion in Dying brought suit in district court arguing that the Washington statute criminalizing assisted suicide was not fair

Holding
Several fundamental rights have been recognized as protected by the due process clause of the Fourteenth Amendment:

- Right to marry
- Right to have children
- Right to education
- Right to privacy in marriage
- Right to contraception
- Right to abortion
- Right to refuse life-sustaining treatment

The state's ban did not violate the Fourteenth Amendment due process clause.

Case

Vacco v. Quill, 117 S.Ct. 2293 (1997)

Issue
Physician-assisted suicide and equal protection

Summary
Physicians and patients argued that New York's statutory ban on assisted suicide violated the equal protection clause of the Fourteenth Amendment.

Holding
The distinction between assisting in suicide and withdrawing life-sustaining treatment is rational and widely recognized in medicine and law. There is no violation of the Constitution.

Right to treatment

Case

Rouse v. Cameron, 125 U.S. App. D.C. 366, 373 F.2d 451 (1966)

Issue

Right to treatment for those adjudicated not guilty by reason of insanity (NGRI)

Summary

Charles Rouse was found NGRI on a misdemeanor charge of carrying a dangerous weapon and was committed to St. Elizabeth's Hospital. He was confined as a dangerously mentally ill patient for four years before filing a writ of habeas corpus in district court. He argued the hospital was not providing him treatment for his mental illness.

Holding

The purpose of involuntary hospitalization is treatment rather than punishment. Habeas corpus was denied but Judge Bazelon:

- Recognized right to treatment for the first time
- Mandated individual treatment plans for patients in hospitals

Case

Wyatt v. Stickney, 344 F.Supp. 387 (M.D. Ala. 1972)

Issue

Right to treatment and the mentally retarded

Summary

Ricky Wyatt was a mentally retarded patient involuntarily confined at Bryce Hospital in Tuscaloosa, Alabama. A class action suit was filed on his behalf alleging poor treatment and deplorable conditions of confinement.

Holding

Bryce Hospital failed to provide a safe and humane environment, a sufficient number of qualified staff, and an individualized treatment plan. Confining a patient without treatment is a violation of due process. Involuntarily committed patients have a constitutional right to:

- Humane psychological and physical environment
- Quality staff in numbers
- Individual treatment plans

Case

Donaldson v. O'Connor, 493 U.S. F.2d 507 (5th Cir. 1974)

Issue
Right to treatment

Summary
Kenneth Donaldson, a man with schizophrenia, was committed to a Florida hospital. He was confined for fourteen years with minimal treatment because he was a Christian Scientist and refused medication and electroconvulsive therapy. Subsequently, the hospital staff denied him access to occupational therapy services and grounds privileges. Donaldson argued that this was malicious.

Holding
The civilly committed patient has a right to an individualized treatment plan.

Case

Estelle v. Gamble, 429 U.S. 97, 97 S.Ct. 285 (1976)

Issue
Deliberate indifference

Summary
J.W. Gamble was an inmate in the Texas Department of Corrections when he claimed to suffer back injuries while performing prison work. Although a prison doctor did prescribe medication, there were a number of staff failures including not filling the prescription for Gamble. Suffering in pain, Gamble refused to work and was brought before the prison disciplinary committee. He filed suit against the director of the Department of Corrections, the prison warden, and the medical director under 42 U.S.C. Section 1983. Gamble claimed that he was subjected to cruel and unusual punishment in violation of the Eighth Amendment.

Holding
"Deliberate indifference to serious medical needs of prisoners" should be the standard for determining whether a violation of the Eighth Amendment exists.

Case

Youngberg v. Romeo, 457 U.S. 307, 102 S.Ct. 2452 (1982)

Issue
Conditions of confinement

Summary

Nicholas Romeo was a profoundly mentally retarded boy who was involuntarily committed to a hospital by his mother. During a two-year time span of hospitalization, Romeo suffered over sixty injuries. A suit was filed against Superintendent Youngberg under the Federal Civil Rights Act of 1964.

Holding

The Fourteenth Amendment does require the State to provide:

- Safe conditions of confinement
- Freedom from bodily restraint
- Right to training

Right to refuse treatment

Case

Superintendent of Belchertown State School v. Saikewicz, 373 Mass. 728, 370 N.E.2d 417 (1977)

Issue

Substituted judgment and treatment of incompetent individuals

Summary

Joseph Saikewicz was a profoundly mentally retarded man at the Belchertown State School, a residence for the mentally retarded in Massachusetts. He was unable to communicate verbally except through gestures and grunts. Saikewicz had an IQ of 10. At 67 years old, he was diagnosed with acute myeloblastic leukemia. Treatment, to which he was not capable of consenting, would only extend his life a matter of weeks. The superintendent of the facility applied for the appointment of a guardian.

Holding

The Court invoked the Substitute Judgment Doctrine, where the judge can make the decision about whether to treat a patient.

Case

Rennie v. Klein, 720 F.2d 266 (3d Cir. 1983)

Issue

Right to refuse antipsychotic medications

Summary

John Rennie had been involuntarily hospitalized for the twelfth time. He instituted a class-action suit asserting a right to refuse antipsychotic medication. The context was that the hospital was understaffed and couldn't do informed consent of polypharmacy.

Holding

The decision to override the patient's right to refuse medication must be the product of the medical authority's professional judgment. The following mandates were in place:

- Written informed consent
- Patient advocates be available to help with informal counsel
- Informal reviews be completed by independent psychiatrists before forcing medications
- Forced medications can be given in emergencies only

Case

Rogers v. Commissioner, 390 Mass. 489, 458 N.E.2d 308 (1983)

Issue

Involuntary commitment and right to refuse medications

Summary

Ruby Rogers was one of seven patients committed to the Boston State Hospital who filed a class-action suit. They challenged the hospital's practice of secluding them and medicating them against their will as a violation of their rights.

Holding

A mentally ill patient committed to a hospital must be considered competent to refuse medication unless otherwise found incompetent before a judge.

chapter fifteen

Children and families

Child abuse reporting

Case

Landeros v. Flood, 17 Cal. 3d 399, 551 P.2d 389 (1976)

Issue
Diagnosis and reporting of battered child syndrome

Summary
Gita Landeros, a baby girl, was repeatedly beaten by her mother at home. When she was 11 months old, Gita was brought to a hospital where doctors found a frightened little girl with a comminuted spiral fracture of the right tibia and fibula, bruises and abrasions over her body, and a nondepressed skull fracture. Dr. Flood neglected to investigate further, missed a diagnosis of battered child syndrome, and released the child into her mother's custody. The infant's suit alleged the defendants committed medical malpractice by failing to make a correct diagnosis, releasing the child to the mother, and failing to notify authorities, thereby proximately causing later injuries.

Holding
There is an expectation that doctors can diagnose child abuse. A doctor is required to possess and exercise, in both diagnosis and treatment, that reasonable degree of knowledge and skill ordinarily possessed and exercised by other members of his profession in similar circumstances.

Case

DeShaney v. Winnebago County Department of Social Services (DSS), 489 U.S. 189, 109 S.Ct. 998 (1989)

Issue
DSS and child protection

Summary
Joshua DeShaney, a little boy, was repeatedly beaten by his father. The Winnebago, Wyoming, DSS was involved but did not have enough evidence

to take custody of the child. When Joshua was 4 years old, his father beat him so severely that Joshua was left profoundly retarded and was confined to an institution for the rest of his life. Joshua's mother sued DSS claiming that they had violated the child's Fourteenth Amendment right.

Holding
The due process clause applies only to state action and not private attacks. Joshua's attacks occurred in privacy and therefore were not DSS' responsibility. The government is not required to take affirmative steps to prevent private attacks.

Child custody and parental competencies

Case

Painter v. Bannister, 258 Iowa 1390, 140 N.W.2d 152 (1966)

Issue
Awarding custody of a minor

Summary
Mr. Painter's wife was killed in a car crash, leaving him the single parent of a 7-year-old boy. Mr. Painter asked the grandparents of his son to care for the boy, but a year later, after Mr. Painter remarried, he wanted his child back. The grandparents refused, arguing that the child was better off in their care (i.e., he was happy, well-adjusted, and was reaching developmental milestones).

Holding
The best interests of child doctrine holds that the important issue is to look at the needs of the child over the needs of the natural parent.

Case

Santosky v. Kramer, 455 U.S. 745, 102 S.Ct. 1388 (1982)

Issue
Termination of parental rights

Summary
This appeal addressed the New York law that if a child appears "neglected," that child is to be removed to an authorized agency (state institution or foster home) and the state's obligation is to attempt to reunite the family. The state can institute "permanent neglect" proceedings to free the child for adoption if deemed appropriate. If there is a finding of permanent

neglect, the parental rights are finally and irrevocably terminated. Such termination denies the parents not only physical custody, but also visitation rights, communication, and the chance to regain custody.

Holding
The fair standard for termination of parental rights is clear and convincing evidence.

Juvenile rights

Case

Gault, In Re, 387 U.S. 1, 87 S.Ct. 1428 (1967)

Issue
Constitutional protections for minors and delinquency proceedings

Summary
Gerald Gault, a 15-year-old already on probation for a minor property offense, was taken into custody by Arizona authorities for making crank phone calls. Gerald was committed as a juvenile delinquent to the State Industrial School for six years. He filed a writ of habeas corpus arguing that the Arizona Juvenile Code violated his due process rights.

Holding
This was the case of a "kangaroo court" that resulted in the criminalization of juvenile court. The United States Supreme Court asserted that juveniles subject to delinquency proceedings should receive broad constitutional protection.

Case

Graham v. Florida, 130 S.Ct. 2011 (2010)

Issue
Juvenile sentencing and the Eighth Amendment

Summary
Terence Graham, 16 years old, was arrested and convicted for attempted robbery in Jacksonville, Florida. He was sentenced to life in prison.

Holding
Sentencing a minor to life in prison without parole for a non-homicide crime violates the Eighth Amendment. Based on *Roper v. Simmons,* juveniles are considered less culpable than adults.

chapter sixteen

Special issues

Sex offenders

Case

Kansas v. Crane, 534 U.S. 407 (2002)

Issue
Sexually violent predators and future dangerousness

Summary
Michael Crane was convicted of lewd and lascivious behavior. Crane's diagnosis was exhibitionism. He pled guilty to aggressive sexual battery and was convicted as a sexually violent predator in Kansas. Crane argued that exhibitionism was not a volitional disorder and therefore the State should have to prove a complete lack of control regarding his potential for future dangerousness.

Holding
The United States Supreme Court rejected Crane's argument.

Case

McKune v. Lile, 536 U.S. 24 (2002)

Issue
Sex offenders and Fifth Amendment rights

Summary
Robert Lile was a convicted sex offender for the rape, sodomy, and kidnapping of a high school student. While in prison, Lile was offered participation in a Sex Abuse Treatment Program (SATP). Participation in the SATP required an admission of guilt, telling of other crimes, and taking a polygraph test, in exchange for placement in lower security, visitation from others, and access to commissary. Lile refused and filed a civil rights claim that the SATP violated his Fifth Amendment right against self-incrimination.

Holding
The SATP serves a vital penological purpose and is therefore acceptable.

Case

Specht v. Patterson, 386 U.S. 605, 87 S.Ct. 1209 (1967)

Issue
Sex offender sentencing

Summary
Francis Specht was convicted in Colorado of a sex offense. The state invoked its Sex Offenders Act to sentence Specht to an indefinite term of detention. Specht filed a writ of habeas corpus challenging his detention.

Holding
The Fourteenth Amendment was violated in this case because Specht did not receive his full rights to due process including notice, hearing, counsel, confrontation of evidence against him, cross-examination of witnesses, and an opportunity to offer his own evidence.

Case

Allen v. Illinois, 478 U.S. 364, 106 S.Ct. 2988 (1986)

Issue
Sexually dangerous persons and the Fifth Amendment

Summary
Terry Allen was arrested and charged with unlawful restraint and deviant sexual assault. Illinois filed a petition to have Allen declared a sexually dangerous person. Allen protested that his Fifth Amendment right was violated.

Holding
The United States Supreme Court held that proceedings under the Illinois Sexually Dangerous Persons Act were civil and not criminal. Therefore, protection against self-incrimination does not apply. Detention under the Sexually Dangerous Persons Act was upheld because the aim is treatment and not punishment.

Case

Kansas v. Hendricks, 117 S.Ct. 2072 (1997)

Issue

Sexually Violent Predator Act

Summary

Leroy Hendricks, diagnosed with pedophilia, had a long history of sexual assault against children. He was serving time in prison for such when Kansas enacted a new Sexually Violent Predator Act. This Act provided civil commitment for persons who were found to have a mental abnormality or personality disorder that predisposed them to violent sexual offenses. Kansas used this Act to commit Hendricks at the end of his prison sentence. Hendricks challenged his continued confinement.

Holding

The Sexually Violent Predator Act did not violate the Constitution. Pedophilia did qualify as a mental disorder. The court rejected Hendrick's argument that his rights (substantive due process, double jeopardy, and ex post facto) were violated.

section 4

Board-style questions

chapter seventeen

Board-style questions

Which of the following cases does not pertain to due process rights of individuals with regard to civil commitment to a psychiatric unit?

a. *Addington v. Texas*
b. *Parham v. J.R.*
c. *Vitek v. Jones*
d. *Rock v. Arkansas*

When did the United States Supreme Court ban the execution of mentally retarded offenders?

a. 1998
b. 2000
c. 2002
d. 2004

Who passed the Prisoner Litigation Reform Act (PLRA)?

a. Joe Biden
b. Bill Clinton
c. Bob Dole
d. Jimmy Carter

Which of the following is not a right for prisoners?

a. Right to marry
b. Right to procreate
c. Right to freedom of speech
d. Right to religious freedom

Which court case raises the issue of scientific reliability?

a. *Mazza v. Huffaker*
b. *Meritor Savings Bank v. Vinson*
c. *Addington v. Texas*
d. *Daubert v. Merrell Dow Pharmaceuticals*

Which case does not address thresholds for admissibility of expert witness testimony in the federal system?

    a. *Daubert v. Merrell Dow Pharmaceuticals*
    b. *General Electric v. Joiner*
    c. *Wyatt v. Stickney*
    d. *Kumho Tire Co. v. Carmichael*

What must be disclosed to an evaluee before a forensic psychiatry evaluation?

    a. Treatment alternatives
    b. Who the forensic psychiatrist is working for
    c. Where the psychiatrist is from
    d. How many cases in which the psychiatrist has testified

Which Amendment right was violated in the case of *Estelle v. Smith*?

    a. Second
    b. Fourth
    c. Sixth
    d. Eighth

Which of the following is not one of the four elements of practice that dictate whether or not a doctor has fallen below the standard of care?

    a. Dereliction
    b. Duty
    c. Diligence
    d. Damage

Which of the following was a California Supreme Court case?

    a. *Bragdon v. Abbott*
    b. *Vacco v. Quill*
    c. *Tarasoff v. Regents of the University of California*
    d. *Rogers v. Commissioner*

Who passed the Health Care Quality Improvement Act?

    a. Ronald Reagan
    b. George W. Bush
    c. Bill Clinton
    d. Barack Obama

Which of the following is not an exception for minors to give consent without the addition of adult or parental consent?

    a. Emancipated minors
    b. Truant minors
    c. Mature minors
    d. Minors being treated for sexually transmitted diseases

What is a factor that increases the risk of undue influence on a testator?

    a. The testator is vulnerable secondary to mental or physical disabilities
    b. The testator is over 65 years of age
    c. The testator has no children
    d. The testator has access to large quantities of money

Which of the following is not a reason an expert might be called in for a deposition?

    a. Verification of expert credentials
    b. Discovery purposes
    c. Expert not being available for trial
    d. Deposition could be used as a tool to impeach an expert with inconsistencies at trial

In a workers' compensation claim there needs to be a causal relationship between employment and what?

    a. Disgruntlement
    b. Harassment
    c. Injury
    d. Death

What qualifies an individual for Social Security Disability Insurance (SSDI)?

    a. An individual must be unable to engage in any substantial gainful act by reason of any medically determinable physical/mental impairment that can lead to death or has lasted more than 6 months
    b. An individual must be unable to engage in any substantial gainful act by reason of any medically determinable physical impairment that can lead to death or has lasted more than 12 months
    c. An individual must be unable to engage in any substantial gainful act by reason of any medically determinable mental impairment that can lead to death or has lasted more than 12 months

d. An individual must be unable to engage in any substantial gainful act by reason of any medically determinable physical/mental
impairment that can lead to death or has lasted more than 12 months

Which of the following is not a component of the Sell criteria?

a. A government interest must be at stake
b. Forced medication furthers a state's interest
c. Medication is the most appropriate way to further a state's interest
d. Medication is readily available

What is false imputation?

a. The complete fabrication of a disorder
b. The purposeful attribution of actual symptoms by an evaluee to an
etiology that he or she knows has no relationship to the development
of such symptoms
c. Purposeful exaggeration of symptoms
d. Feigning magical powers

The "threshold model for consideration of malingering" includes psychiatric and physical symptoms accompanied by which of the following?

a. Voluntary control over symptoms
b. Subtle complaints
c. Good response to treatment
d. Compliance with treatment

Which of the following is not an atypical hallucination suggestive of possible malingering?

a. Auditory hallucinations that are continuous and incessant with
no breaks
b. Auditory hallucinations that include voices from the evaluee's mother
c. Visual hallucinations in black and white
d. Feeling fingernails grow during an evaluation

Which of the following is a psychiatric diagnosis most closely associated
with risk of future violence?

a. Borderline personality disorder
b. Paranoid personality disorder
c. Narcissistic personality disorder
d. Antisocial personality disorder

Which tool is used to assess the risk of recidivism in sex offenders?

a. TOMM
b. GCCT
c. HCR-20
d. Static-99

What adverse medication side effect was the impetus for the case in *Clites v. Iowa*?

a. Suicide
b. Parkinson's disease
c. Diabetes
d. Tardive dyskinesia

What was the issue in the case of *Kaimowitz v. Michigan Department of Mental Health*?

a. Informed consent
b. Forced medication
c. Right to treatment
d. Duty to protect

What was the "related service" at issue in the case of *Irving Independent School District v. Tatro*?

a. Catheterization
b. Ambulation
c. Visual guidance
d. Education

What duty was the therapist found negligent of in the case of *Peck v. Counseling Service of Addison County, Inc.*?

a. Duty to diagnose
b. Duty to protect
c. Duty to evaluate
d. Duty to treat

What is the standard of proof for civil commitment?

a. More likely than not
b. Preponderance of the evidence
c. Clear and convincing evidence
d. Beyond a reasonable doubt

Lessard v. Schmidt was decided in which court of law?

    a. United States Supreme Court
    b. Appellate court
    c. Trial court
    d. Federal court

What important concept was presented by Judge Bazelon in the case of *Lake v. Cameron*?

    a. Least restrictive alternative for treatment
    b. Right to refuse treatment
    c. Importance of informed consent
    d. Criminalization of civil commitment

Which case recognized the patient's right to individualized treatment plans?

    a. *Vacco v. Quill*
    b. *Rogers v. Commissioner*
    c. *Rouse v. Cameron*
    d. *Cruzan v. Director, Missouri DMH*

What was the standard of proof that was established in the case of *Cruzan v. Director, Missouri DMH*?

    a. Probable cause
    b. Preponderance of the evidence
    c. Clear and convincing evidence
    d. Beyond a reasonable doubt

Which of the following was not a finding of the court in the case of *Rennie v. Klein*?

    a. Patients must provide written informed consent
    b. Forced medications are acceptable at the discretion of doctors
    c. Advocates in the form of legal counsel must be made available to patients refusing treatment
    d. Forced medications are acceptable in emergency situations

What was the defining issue in the case of *Burlington Industries v. Ellerth*?

    a. Conduct
    b. Damages
    c. Intent
    d. Restitution

Which United States Supreme Court case was the first to address sexual harassment as a cause of action?

  a. *Oncale v. Sundowners Offshore Services*
  b. *Gebser v. Lago Vista Independent School District*
  c. *Harris v. Forklift Systems, Inc.*
  d. *Meritor Savings Bank v. Vinson*

Which Amendment right was in question in the case of *Vacco v. Quill*?

  a. First
  b. Sixth
  c. Eighth
  d. Fourteenth

Vermont Law 114 was found to violate what act in the case of *Hargrave v. Vermont*?

  a. Americans with Disabilities Act
  b. Patriot Act
  c. Affordable Care Act
  d. Social Security Act

In the case of *Pennsylvania Department of Corrections v. Yeskey*, what medical condition precluded Yeskey from participating in boot camp?

  a. Asthma
  b. Hypertension
  c. Diabetes
  d. Obesity

What major life activity was the issue in the case of *Bragdon v. Abbott*?

  a. Breathing
  b. Toileting
  c. Eating
  d. Reproducing

What United States Supreme Court case held that a contagious disease is a physical impairment?

  a. *Bragdon v. Abbott*
  b. *Sutton v. United Airlines, Inc.*
  c. *School Board of Nassau County Florida v. Arline*
  d. *Toyota Manufacturing Company v. Williams*

What Amendment right was violated in the case of *Graham v. Florida*?

  a. First
  b. Sixth
  c. Eighth
  d. Fourteenth

The case of *Fare v. Michael C.* dealt with what juvenile rights?

  a. Right to refuse treatment
  b. Miranda rights
  c. Right to testify
  d. Right to treatment

Which Amendment right was in question in the case of *McKeiver v. Pennsylvania*?

  a. First
  b. Sixth
  c. Eighth
  d. Fourteenth

What is the standard established by the United States Supreme Court for all delinquency adjudication?

  a. Reason to believe
  b. Preponderance of the evidence
  c. Clear and convincing evidence
  d. Beyond a reasonable doubt

All of the following are "Determinative Factors" in deciding a judicial waiver (i.e., trying a juvenile as an adult in court) except:

  a. Minor offense
  b. Personal circumstances
  c. Public safety
  d. Likelihood of rehabilitation

Which case determined that a state law requiring two-parent notification of a minor's intent to have an abortion was unconstitutional?

  a. *Planned Parenthood v. Danforth*
  b. *H.L. v. Matheson*
  c. *Carey v. Population Services International*
  d. *Hodgson v. Minnesota*

What special group was granted authority to admit minors to a psychiatric hospital in the case of *Parham v. J.L. and J.R.?*

   a. Parents
   b. Teachers
   c. Police officers
   d. Firefighters

What was the basis for the court's decision in the case of *Painter v. Bannister?*

   a. Preponderance of the evidence
   b. Clear and convincing evidence
   c. Beyond a reasonable doubt
   d. Best interest of the child

Which Amendment right was at issue in the case of *Maryland v. Craig?*

   a. First
   b. Sixth
   c. Eighth
   d. Fourteenth

What was the standard for termination of parental rights in the case of *Santosky v. Kramer?*

   a. Preponderance of the evidence
   b. Clear and convincing evidence
   c. Beyond a reasonable doubt
   d. Best interest of the child

In the case of *Landeros v. Flood,* doctors are expected to be able to diagnose what in children?

   a. Seizure
   b. Child abuse
   c. Meningitis
   d. Cancer

In the case of *Hoffman v. Harris,* who was sued?

   a. Doctors
   b. Hospital administration
   c. Nurses
   d. Social workers

What man was the catalyst for the Sexual Predator Law in Washington?

    a. Earl Shriner
    b. Adam Walsh
    c. Jesse Timmendequas
    d. Jacob Wetterling

Which Amendment right was in question in the case of *Washington v. Glucksberg*?

    a. First
    b. Sixth
    c. Eighth
    d. Fourteenth

Which Amendment is most commonly challenged in Megan's Law?

    a. First
    b. Fifth
    c. Eighth
    d. Fourteenth

Which Amendment right was challenged in the case of *Allen v. Illinois*?

    a. Fourth
    b. Fifth
    c. Eighth
    d. Fourteenth

Which Amendment right was violated in the case of *Specht v. Patterson*?

    a. Fourth
    b. Sixth
    c. Eighth
    d. Fourteenth

Which Amendment right was challenged in the case of *McKune v. Lile*?

    a. Fifth
    b. Sixth
    c. Eighth
    d. Fourteenth

In the case of *Kansas v. Crane*, what was the diagnosis given to Michael Crane?

   a. Schizophrenia
   b. Bipolar
   c. Exhibitionism
   d. Impulse control disorder

What was the issue considered in the case of *Frendak v. U.S.*?

   a. Competency
   b. Criminal responsibility
   c. Amnestic disorders
   d. Truancy

The case of *Foucha v. Louisiana* established that persons adjudicated insane cannot be held in psychiatric institutions unless they are found mentally ill and what else?

   a. Incompetent
   b. Noncompliant
   c. Dangerous
   d. Isolated

Which of the following is the Dusky Standard for competency to stand trial?

   a. A defendant has the sufficient present ability to consult with a lawyer and have a rational and factual understanding of the case
   b. A defendant had the sufficient ability to consult with a lawyer and have a rational and factual understanding of the case at the time of the crime
   c. A defendant has the sufficient present ability to consult with their doctor and have a rational and factual understanding of their illness
   d. A defendant has some ability to consult with a lawyer and have a rational and factual understanding of the case

Which of the following cases did not deal with hypnotically refreshed memories?

   a. *Rock v. Arkansas*
   b. *People v. Shirley*
   c. *Riggins v. Nevada*
   d. *State v. Hurd*

Which Amendment right was not in question in the case of *Rock v. Arkansas*?

a. Fifth
b. Sixth
c. Eighth
d. Fourteenth

Which of the following is not one of Dr. Orne's safeguards to hypnotically refreshed memories?

a. Hypnotists should be hired by the prosecution
b. Before hypnosis, the therapist should take a thorough history of the alleged events
c. Hypnotism sessions should be video-recorded
d. Only the hypnotist and subject should be present during the session

What is a slang phrase for the diminished capacity defense?

a. "Out of luck defense"
b. "Drunk as a skunk defense"
c. "Twinkie defense"
d. "Win some lose some defense"

Which of the following is a sign of impairment from a mental condition according to the Social Security Act?

a. Marked restrictions in life activities of daily living
b. Limited social functioning
c. Repeated episodes of decompensation in work only
d. Oversleeping for work

In the case of *Montana v. Egelhoff*, excessive intake of what substance was the basis for a diminished capacity defense?

a. Cocaine
b. Sweets
c. Ecstasy
d. Alcohol

What is an Alford plea?

a. Pleading no contest while protesting innocence
b. Pleading for mercy from the court
c. Entering into a plea bargain while protesting innocence
d. Pleading guilty but asking the court to consider mitigating factors for a reduced sentence

Which of the following is a status crime?

    a. Theft
    b. Homelessness
    c. Assault
    d. Murder

What was "Operation Baxstrom"?

    a. The transport of sexual offenders from prison cells into solitary confinement
    b. The release of a large number of inmates into the community
    c. The mass transit of felony offenders to securely locked facilities
    d. The permanent closure of long-term psychiatric facilities

According to the Jessica Lunsford Act, child molesters in the state of Florida are required to wear or carry what?

    a. Orange jumpsuits
    b. Scarlet letter
    c. GPS tracking device
    d. Identification card

In the case of *Riggins v. Nevada*, the United States Supreme Court opined that the state is obligated to establish what when treating prisoners with psychotropic medications?

    a. Duty
    b. Benefit
    c. Alternatives
    d. Need

What Amendment right was in question in the case of *Washington v. Harper*?

    a. Fourth
    b. Fifth
    c. Sixth
    d. Fourteenth

What is the meaning of the "Bell test"?

    a. A pretrial detainee can be subjected to any conditions
    b. A pretrial detainee cannot be subjected to conditions that are disproportionate to their accused crime

c. A pretrial detainee cannot be subjected to conditions that are not reasonably related to a legitimate government interest
d. A pretrial detainee cannot be subjected to conditions that could lead to physical or mental deterioration

What was the issue in the case of *State v. Perry*?

a. Treatment of a defendant to restore them to competency for trial
b. Forcibly medicating a defendant pleading not guilty by reason of insanity
c. Treatment of a prisoner deemed incompetent to be executed
d. Transfer of a prisoner to a psychiatric institution

Which Act did President Obama sign into law only five days after taking office?

a. Affordable Health Care Act
b. Unlocking Consumer Choice and Wireless Competition Act
c. Lilly Ledbetter Fair Pay Act
d. Veterans Health Care Budget Reform and Transparency Act

What was the issue in the case of *Panetti v. Quarterman*?

a. Competence to stand trial
b. Competence to be executed
c. Competence to provide informed consent
d. Competence to hold a driver's license

Which Amendment right was questioned in the case of *Ford v. Wainwright*?

a. First
b. Fourth
c. Sixth
d. Eighth

Which United States Supreme Court Justice suggested an "execution competency standard"?

a. Justice Powell
b. Justice O'Connor
c. Justice Roberts
d. Justice Scalia

Which Amendment right was in question in the case of *Ring v. Arizona*?

a. First
b. Fourth
c. Sixth
d. Eighth

What was the issue in the case of *Payne v. Tennessee*?

a. Competence
b. Victim impact statements
c. Hearsay
d. Child witness testimony

What controversial testimony was provided by Dr. Grigson in the case of *Barefoot v. Estelle*?

a. Hypothetical questions
b. Hearsay evidence
c. Hypnotically refreshed memories
d. Unqualified testimony

In the case of *In re Gault*, the United States Supreme Court said that in hearings that could potentially lead to the institutionalization of juveniles, they had a right to all of the following except:

a. Notice of charges
b. Trial by jury
c. Legal counsel
d. Privilege against self-incrimination

Which two Amendment rights were questioned in the case of *Estelle v. Smith*?

a. First and Fourth
b. Fourth and Fifth
c. Fifth and Sixth
d. Eighth and Fourteenth

Which two Amendment rights were questioned in the case of *Roper v. Simmons*?

a. First and Fourth
b. Fourth and Fifth
c. Fifth and Sixth
d. Eighth and Fourteenth

Which United States Supreme Court Justice suggested an "evolving standard of decency" with regard to the death penalty and mental retardation?

a. Justice Powell
b. Justice O'Connor
c. Justice Roberts
d. Justice Scalia

In 2002, what was the evidence that Americans did not support the death penalty of individuals with mental retardation?

a. Best guess
b. Brief questionnaire
c. Polling data
d. AMA directive

What type of discrimination was the basis for the argument in the case of *McCleskey v. Kemp*?

a. Racial
b. Sexual
c. Age
d. Disability

Which Federal Rule of Evidence was cited in the rationale for the United States Supreme Court's decision in the case of *Jaffee v. Redmond*?

a. 402
b. 501
c. 601
d. 702

There are two exceptions cited in the case *Canterbury v. Spence* as to the physician's responsibility to employ the objective standard and provide patients with informed consent. Which of the following is one of those exceptions?

a. Full disclosure of risks would undoubtedly cause the patient to reject the treatment recommendation
b. The physician is an intern and therefore, not yet fully qualified to obtain informed consent
c. The situation is an emergency
d. The adverse risk is so rare that it is nearly negligible

What is the protection guaranteed under the First Amendment?

    a. Freedom of speech
    b. Freedom from unreasonable search and seizure
    c. Proscription of cruel and unusual punishment
    d. Right to due process

In the case of *Jablonski v. U.S.*, which was not one of the malpractice claims raised against Dr. Kopiloff (the doctor who failed to hospitalize the very dangerous Jablonski)?

    a. Failure to protect
    b. Failure to get past medical records
    c. Failure to warn
    d. Failure to give antipsychotics

What was the legal issue in the case of *Naidu v. Laird*?

    a. Confidentiality and privilege
    b. Informed consent
    c. Duty to protect
    d. Expert testimony

What is the name of the test that considers "admissibility of scientific evidence based on general acceptance of the methodology by the scientific community"?

    a. Daubert test
    b. Reliability test
    c. Joiner test
    d. Frye test

What qualifies as being in the "zone of danger" for psychic injury claims?

    a. Not being harmed but being personally endangered by an act
    b. Being physically harmed but not as severely as others by an act
    c. Witnessing from afar an act but having no threat to your body
    d. Hearing about a significant event that leads to emotional harm

What is the test for sexual harassment, as the court ruled in *Meritor Savings Bank v. Vinson*?

    a. Involuntary participation in sex acts
    b. Unwelcome sexual advancements

c. Feeling physically threatened
d. Constant ridicule and insult

Under which Title did Vinson file suit against Meritor Savings Bank for the constant harassment by her boss?

a. Title V
b. Title VII
c. Title VIII
d. Title X

Why was Dr. Hartogs found guilty of medical malpractice in the case of *Roy v. Hartogs*?

a. Improper prescribing
b. Failing to provide informed consent
c. Inadequate documentation
d. Sex with his patient

What was the basis for the court's original determination that Milton Dusky was competent to stand trial?

a. Ability to assist in his own defense
b. Orientation
c. Rational and factual understanding of the case
d. Full knowledge of courtroom procedures

When a court is considering whether or not amnesia precludes a defendant from being competent to stand trial, as in the case of *Wilson v. U.S.*, which of the following is not a factor that the court should consider?

a. Extent to which amnesia affected the defendant's ability to consult with a lawyer
b. Extent to which amnesia affected the defendant's ability to testify on their behalf
c. Extent to which the government could assist the defendant and counsel in reconstruction of the event
d. Strength of the defense's case

Leroy Hendricks was confined in Kansas beyond his prison sentence for sexual offenses due to his mental disorder and high likelihood of recidivism of predatory sexual acts. He challenged his confinement on the basis of all of the following except which?

a. Substantive due process
b. Double jeopardy
c. Right to confront accuser
d. Ex post facto

In the case of *Colorado v. Connelly*, Chief Justice Rehnquist wrote for the majority of the United States Supreme Court and restricted the concept of voluntary confession to mean only that the confession was made without all of the following except:

a. Intimidation
b. Coercion
c. Encouragement
d. Deception

What standard for competency to stand trial was established by the case of *Cooper v. Oklahoma*?

a. Best guess
b. Preponderance of the evidence
c. Clear and convincing evidence
d. Beyond a reasonable doubt

What is the test for insanity in a criminal case?

a. Dusky Standard
b. M'Naghten's Rule
c. Reasonable Person
d. Strict Scrutiny

What are the requirements to hold an insanity acquittee in a psychiatric hospital according to the holding in *Foucha v. Louisiana*?

a. Mentally ill and dangerous
b. Mentally ill and disabled
c. Mentally ill and amnestic
d. Mentally ill and refusing treatment

Which of the following is not an actuarial risk assessment for violence?

a. HCR-20
b. TOMM

   c. VRAG
   d. Psychopathy checklist

When was the first execution of a juvenile offender?

   a. 1642
   b. 1742
   c. 1842
   d. 1942

What Amendment rights did Vickie Rock argue were taken from her when an Arkansas court refused to allow testimony of her hypnotically refreshed memories?

   a. First, Fourth, Fifth
   b. Fourth, Fifth, Sixth
   c. Fifth, Sixth, Fourteenth
   d. Sixth, Eighth, Fourteenth

In the case of *Atkins v. Virginia*, which Amendment right was challenged in the sentencing of the mentally retarded man, Daryl Atkins, to death by execution?

   a. Fourth
   b. Sixth
   c. Eighth
   d. Fourteenth

In the case of *Roper v. Simmons*, the United States Supreme Court opined that execution of a minor violated which Amendments?

   a. Fourth and Eighth
   b. Sixth and Eighth
   c. Sixth and Fourteenth
   d. Eighth and Fourteenth

What was the Louisiana Supreme Court's opinion regarding medicating a person with the purpose to achieve competence for execution?

   a. They were in favor when the crime was so heinous that it served a legitimate government interest
   b. They were in favor when victim impact statements compelled a jury to rule in favor of medication to achieve competence for execution

c. They were against this as a matter of the Constitution
d. They were against as a matter of expense and financial burden to the state

Which case is the origin for informed consent?

a. *Salgo v. Leland Stanford Junior University Board of Trustees*
b. *Natanson v. Kline*
c. *Canterbury v. Spence*
d. *Schloendorff v. Society of N.Y. Hospital*

In the case of *Ford v. Wainwright*, which Justice suggested an Execution Competency Standard?

a. Justice Rehnquist
b. Justice Powell
c. Justice O'Connor
d. Justice Scalia

The Wetterling Act imposes stringent registration programs for sex offenders. This includes that in all states sex offenders must register for how many years?

a. 5
b. 10
c. 15
d. 20

What are the two mens rea for reckless behaviors that qualify under deliberate indifference?

a. Subjective and objective recklessness
b. Retrospective and prospective recklessness
c. Inherent and obvious recklessness
d. Criminal and procedural recklessness

What is the meaning of the "standard of care" for physicians?

a. The physician is required to possess and exercise that reasonable skill and knowledge ordinarily possessed and exercised by other members of his profession in all circumstances
b. The physician is required to possess and exercise that reasonable skill and knowledge ordinarily possessed and exercised by other members of his profession in similar circumstances

c. The physician is required to possess and exercise that reasonable skill and knowledge always possessed and exercised by elite members of his profession in similar circumstances
d. The physician is required to possess and exercise that perfect skill and knowledge always possessed and exercised by other members of his profession in similar circumstances

By what standard must the state prove its case before there is a finding of permanent neglect so that parental rights are terminated?

a. Parental rights can never be fully terminated
b. Preponderance of the evidence
c. Clear and convincing evidence
d. Beyond a reasonable doubt

What does SORNA stand for?

a. Serial Offender Registry and Notification Act
b. Sexual Offender Registry and Notification Act
c. Substance Offender Registry and Notification Act
d. Serious Offender Registry and Notification Act

Fifteen-year-old Gerald Gault argued that what was violated when he was taken into custody for making crank phone calls and sentenced to the State Industrial School for six years?

a. Right to freedom of speech
b. Right to be silent
c. Right against self-incrimination
d. Right to due process

What was 16-year-old Terence Graham's sentence after being convicted of attempted robbery in Florida?

a. Life in prison
b. 1 year in prison
c. 5 years in prison
d. 10 years in prison

What were the requests of the Sexual Abuse Treatment Program (SATP) that was offered to Robert Lile while in prison for a sex offense?

a. Admission of responsibility
b. Hormonal treatment

c. Disclosure of partners in crime

d. Psychiatric admission

Which Act did Graydon Comstock argue was unconstitutional in that it contributed to his indefinite detention in prison?

a. Jessica Lunsford Act

b. Wetterling Act

c. Kanka Act

d. Adam Walsh Act

Which Amendment right was in question in the case of *Specht v. Patterson*?

a. Fifth

b. Sixth

c. Eighth

d. Fourteenth

Considering the case of *Kansas v. Hendricks*, what was the diagnosis of Leroy Hendricks?

a. Antisocial personality

b. Impulse control disorder

c. Psychosis

d. Pedophilia

Who passed the Prison Rape Elimination Act?

a. Ronald Reagan

b. Bill Clinton

c. George W. Bush

d. Barack Obama

Operation Baxstrom, the release of a large number of civilly committed patients into the community, was the direct result of Johnnie Baxstrom's unfair civil commitment following the end of his penal sentence. His commitment was unfair because it violated which Amendment right?

a. Fifth

b. Sixth

c. Seventh

d. Fourteenth

Which court decided the case of *Lessard v. Schmidt*?

a. United States Supreme Court
b. District Appeals Court
c. Superior Court
d. Trial Court

Who argued in the *American Bar Association Journal* that treatment serves a quid pro quo justification for hospitalization?

a. Dr. Morton Brinbaum
b. Justice O'Connor
c. Justice Rehnquist
d. Dr. Benjamin Rush

What illness was recognized as qualifying for disability in the case of *Bragdon v. Abbott*?

a. Tuberculosis
b. Myopia
c. Spina bifida
d. HIV

chapter eighteen

Board-style questions and answers

Which of the following cases does not pertain to due process rights of individuals with regard to civil commitment to a psychiatric unit?

   a. *Addington v. Texas*
   b. *Parham v. J.R.*
   c. *Vitek v. Jones*
   d. *Rock v. Arkansas*

Answer: d

Addington v. Texas established the burden of proof for civil commitment to a psychiatric facility as clear and convincing evidence.

   Parham v. J.R. granted parental commitment of a child to a psychiatric facility with two safeguards:

* Approval by a psychiatrist
* Periodic review

Vitek v. Jones upheld that prisoners could not be transferred to a psychiatric facility without safeguards:

* Adequate notice
* Adversarial hearing
* Written findings
* Availability of legal counsel

Rock v. Arkansas involved the admittance of hypnotically refreshed memories into testimony.

When did the United States Supreme Court ban the execution of mentally retarded offenders?

   a. 1998
   b. 2000
   c. 2002
   d. 2004

Answer: c

The United States Supreme Court banned execution of the mentally retarded in June 2002 with its ruling on the case *Atkins v. Virginia*. The holding was that the standard of decency had evolved and now there was polling data to show that Americans did not support the death penalty for individuals with mental retardation.

Who passed the Prisoner Litigation Reform Act (PLRA)?

    a. Joe Biden
    b. Bill Clinton
    c. Bob Dole
    d. Jimmy Carter

Answer: c

The Act was passed by Senator Dole in 1996. The Act applies to all inmates who file civil litigation under Section 1983 and it serves to discourage frivolous lawsuits by imposing severe restrictions such as:

- File-fee payments
- Court screening of complaints
- Prohibition against filing a Section 1983 until other suits are exhausted
- Restricting nonmonetary relief
- Prohibiting the court from awarding attorney fees
- Three strikes you're out policy (inmates cannot file more than three Section 1983 suits).

Which of the following is not a right for prisoners?

    a. Right to marry
    b. Right to procreate
    c. Right to freedom of speech
    d. Right to religious freedom

Answer: b

Prisoners do not have the right to vote, rehabilitation services, drug and alcohol treatment, or procreation.

   Gerber v. Hickman was a case where an inmate wanted to FedEx his sperm to his partner for insemination. The court struck this down and said that prisoners did not have a constitutional right to procreate.

Which court case raises the issue of scientific reliability?

    a. *Mazza v. Huffaker*
    b. *Meritor Savings Bank v. Vinson*
    c. *Addington v. Texas*
    d. *Daubert v. Merrell Dow Pharmaceuticals*

Answer: d

Daubert v. Merrell Dow Pharmaceuticals was the case that established the criteria to help determine scientific reliability. First, whether specific techniques or theory could be tested. Second, whether they had been subjected to public scrutiny via peer review or publication. Third, whether there was an acceptable rate of error. Finally, if the technique or theory was accepted in the scientific community.

Mazza v. Huffaker is a case that dealt with liability to patients. The outcome was that public policy does not preclude coverage under medical malpractice for negligence in abandoning a patient.

Meritor Savings Bank v. Vinson dealt with sexual harassment. The court held that hostile claims are actionable under Title VII when the conduct in question is severe.

Addington v. Texas established the standard of proof in civil commitment hearings as clear and convincing evidence.

Which case does not address thresholds for admissibility of expert witness testimony in the federal system?

   a. *Daubert v. Merrell Dow Pharmaceuticals*
   b. *General Electric v. Joiner*
   c. *Wyatt v. Stickney*
   d. *Kumho Tire Co v. Carmichael*

Answer: c
All of these cases address thresholds for admissibility in the federal system except *Wyatt v. Stickney*, which dealt with the right to psychiatric treatment. This suit was filed on behalf of patients at Bryce Hospital in Tuscaloosa, Alabama. About five thousand patients were involuntarily committed at Bryce Hospital and subjected to deplorable conditions including lack of treatment, which was considered a violation of their due process. In this case the court held that involuntarily committed patients should get three things:

   • Humane psychiatric and physical environment
   • Quality staff in numbers
   • Individualized treatment plans

What must be disclosed to an evaluee before a forensic psychiatry evaluation?

   a. Treatment alternatives
   b. Who the forensic psychiatrist is working for
   c. Where the psychiatrist is from
   d. How many cases in which the psychiatrist has testified

Answer: b

Prior to conducting an evaluation for forensic psychiatry purposes, there are several things that must be disclosed which include the following:

- The purpose of the evaluation
- Whom the psychiatrist is conducting the evaluation for
- The fact that the psychiatrist is not a "treating doctor"
- What the psychiatrist intends to do with the information gathered from the interview
- The fact that the opinions formed might or might not help the evaluee's case

Which Amendment right was violated in the case of *Estelle v. Smith*?

a. Second
b. Fourth
c. Sixth
d. Eighth

Answer: c

A forensic psychiatrist should not evaluate a defendant—if they were retained by opposing counsel—until that individual has consulted with his or her defense attorney. The Sixth Amendment right was violated in *Estelle v. Smith* because the evaluee was interviewed prior to having a chance to be advised by counsel.

Which of the following is not one of the four elements of practice that dictate whether or not a doctor has fallen below the standard of care?

a. Dereliction
b. Duty
c. Diligence
d. Damage

Answer: c

The standard of care is a legal term that defines the standard against which allegations of negligence are measured. Falling below the standard means that there was a dereliction of duty that directly led to damage.

Which of the following was a California Supreme Court case?

a. *Bragdon v. Abbott*
b. *Vacco v. Quill*
c. *Tarasoff v. Regents of the University of California*
d. *Rogers v. Commissioner*

Answer: c

The Tarasoff case was a California Supreme Court case that articulated a new element to the standard of care. Psychiatrists and psychologists have a duty to protect foreseeably endangered persons from violent patients.

Bragdon v. Abbott dealt with the issue of whether or not HIV is covered by the Americans with Disabilities Act.

Vacco v. Quill dealt with the right to physician-assisted suicide in the state of New York. The United States Supreme Court held that New York's statute banning physician-assisted suicide did not violate the equal protection clause of the Fourteenth Amendment.

Rogers v. Commissioner was a Massachusetts case that held that committed patients remain competent to make treatment decisions until the patient is adjudicated as incompetent by a judge.

Who passed the Health Care Quality Improvement Act?

    a. Ronald Reagan
    b. George W. Bush
    c. Bill Clinton
    d. Barack Obama

Answer: a

In 1986 the United States Congress passed and President Reagan signed the Health Care Quality Improvement Act, which forever changed a doctor's risk of liability. The Act required all healthcare entities to report not only findings of malpractice but also any professional disciplinary actions that had adversely affected the respondent physician's membership in that healthcare entity.

The legislation had the following outcomes:

- Set up a National Practitioner Data Bank
- Mandated reporting of malpractice claims
- Mandated reporting of M.D. disciplinary action
- Protected doctors engaged in the peer review

Which of the following is not an exception for minors to give consent without the addition of adult or parental consent?

    a. Emancipated minors
    b. Truant minors
    c. Mature minors
    d. Minors being treated for sexually transmitted diseases

Answer: b

Truant minors are not allowed to provide consent without parental permission. Although parents are generally the decision-makers for minors, there are exceptions such as those mentioned above. The case that established that mature minors are able to give consent was *Bellotti v. Baird* in 1979.

What is a factor that increases the risk of undue influence on a testator?

    a. The testator is vulnerable secondary to mental or physical disabilities
    b. The testator is over 65 years of age
    c. The testator has no children
    d. The testator has access to large quantities of money

Answer: a
There are several factors considered by courts to increase the risk of undue influence:

- The testator was particularly vulnerable because of dependencies or mental or physical disabilities
- The influencer increased the testator's level of perceived helplessness
- The influencer kept others away from the testator
- The influencer brought the testator to an attorney of the influencer's choosing and was present during the drawing up of the will
- The influencer isolated the testator from news of friends and family
- The influencer actively misled the testator about other potential beneficiaries
- The undue influence caused an unnatural disposition of the property

Which of the following is not a reason an expert might be called in for a deposition?

    a. Verification of expert credentials
    b. Discovery purposes
    c. Expert not being available for trial
    d. Deposition could be used as a tool to impeach expert with inconsistencies at trial

Answer: a
All of the above are reasons for an expert being called for a deposition except for a. During a deposition the opposing counsel will require the expert to state and clarify his or her opinions and to describe the basis for those opinions.

In a workers' compensation claim there needs to be a causal relationship between employment and what?

    a. Disgruntlement
    b. Harassment

c. Injury
d. Death

Answer: c
Workers' compensation is an administration remedy designed as an alternate to filing other types of claims. It is a "no fault" system where a finding of fault is not required. It requires that there be a causal relationship between employment and injury or disability.

What qualifies an individual for Social Security Disability Insurance (SSDI)?

a. An individual must be unable to engage in any substantial gainful act by reason of any medically determinable physical/mental impairment that can lead to death or has lasted more than 6 months
b. An individual must be unable to engage in any substantial gainful act by reason of any medically determinable physical impairment that can lead to death or has lasted more than 12 months
c. An individual must be unable to engage in any substantial gainful act by reason of any medically determinable mental impairment that can lead to death or has lasted more than 12 months
d. An individual must be unable to engage in any substantial gainful act by reason of any medically determinable physical/mental impairment that can lead to death or has lasted more than 12 months

Answer: d
To qualify for SSDI, an individual must be unable to engage in any substantial gainful act by reason of any medically determinable physical/mental impairment that can lead to death or has lasted more than 12 months. A mental disorder itself does not automatically equate to disability. Disability is assessed by medical and nonmedical means. The determination of disability requires more than a medical consideration of symptoms and health status.

Which of the following is not a component of the Sell criteria?

a. A government interest must be at stake
b. Forced medication furthers a state's interest
c. Medication is the most appropriate way to further a state's interest
d. Medication is readily available

Answer: d
The Sell criteria was established in 2003 after a St. Louis dentist, Dr. Sell, was found incompetent to stand trial for Medicaid fraud due to delusions. The United States Supreme Court allowed for the use of forced medications to restore competency to stand trial but established strict criteria that first must be met. These included (1) a government interest being at

stake, (2) forced medications must further a state's interest, (3) medication is the most appropriate way to further a state's interest, and (4) the use of medication is medically appropriate.

What is false imputation?

a. The complete fabrication of a disorder
b. The purposeful attribution of actual symptoms by an evaluee to an etiology that he or she knows has no relationship to the development of such symptoms
c. Purposeful exaggeration of symptoms
d. Feigning magical powers

Answer: b
The complete fabrication of a disorder is pure malingering. The purposeful exaggeration of symptoms is partial malingering. False imputation is the purposeful attribution of actual symptoms by an evaluee to an etiology that he or she knows has no relationship to the development of such symptoms.

The "threshold model for consideration of malingering" includes psychiatric and physical symptoms accompanied by which of the following?

a. Voluntary control over symptoms
b. Subtle complaints
c. Good response to treatment
d. Compliance with treatment

Answer: a
According to the model proposed by Cunnien in 1997, malingering should be suspected when psychological or physical symptoms are accompanied by:

• Suspicion of voluntary control over symptoms, atypical symptomatic fluctuation, or an unusual symptomatic response to treatment
• Atypical presentation in the presence of environmental incentives or noxious environmental conditions
• Complaints grossly in excess of clinical findings
• Substantial noncompliance with treatment

Which of the following is not an atypical hallucination suggestive of possible malingering?

a. Auditory hallucinations that are continuous and incessant with no breaks
b. Auditory hallucinations that include voices from the evaluee's mother

  c. Visual hallucinations in black and white
  d. Feeling fingernails grow during an evaluation

Answer: b
The following are some atypical hallucinations that may suggest malingering:

- Auditory hallucinations that are continuous rather than intermittent
- Auditory hallucinations that are vague or inaudible
- Auditory hallucinations that are spoken in stilted language
- Lack of strategies on the part of the evaluee to diminish auditory hallucinations
- Visual hallucinations that are seen in black and white
- Hallucinations that are not associated with a delusion

Which of the following is a psychiatric diagnosis most closely associated with risk of future violence?

  a. Borderline personality disorder
  b. Paranoid personality disorder
  c. Narcissistic personality disorder
  d. Antisocial personality disorder

Answer: d
Antisocial personality disorder is most closely associated with a risk of future violence.

Which tool is used to assess the risk of recidivism in sex offenders?

  a. TOMM
  b. GCCT
  c. HCR-20
  d. Static-99

Answer: d
The Static-99 is a tool to assess the risk of recidivism in sex offenders. The TOMM (Test of Memory Malingering) is used to assess malingering. The GCCT (Georgia Court Competency Test) is used to assess competence to stand trial. The HCR-20 (a 20-item test scoring historical, clinical, and risk factors) assesses future risk of violence.

What adverse medication side effect was the impetus for the case in *Clites v. Iowa*?

  a. Suicide
  b. Parkinson's disease

c. Diabetes
d. Tardive dyskinesia

Answer: d
Clites v. Iowa was a Court of Appeals case where the parents of Timothy Clites sued after their son was given neuroleptics in a state hospital and developed tardive dyskinesia. This was the first appellate case affirming the need for informed consent of patients to avoid paying for damages from adverse side effects such as tardive dyskinesia.

What was the issue in the case of *Kaimowitz v. Michigan Department of Mental Health*?

a. Informed consent
b. Forced medication
c. Right to treatment
d. Duty to protect

Answer: a
Mr. Louis Smith was committed to a hospital in 1955 and diagnosed as a sexual psychopath. A research study looking at uncontrolled aggression enrolled Smith with the agreement of himself and his parents. Later, Mr. Kaimowitz took action with the Michigan court claiming that it is impossible to obtain truly informed consent from an institutionalized patient.

What was the "related service" at issue in the case of *Irving Independent School District v. Tatro*?

a. Catheterization
b. Ambulation
c. Visual guidance
d. Education

Answer: a
Irving Independent School District v. Tatro raised the issue of education-related services. Amber Tatro was a student with spina bifida who required catheterization. The Court held that under the Education for All Handicapped Children Act, "related services" included catheterization.

What duty was the therapist found negligent of in the case of *Peck v. Counseling Service of Addison County, Inc.*?

a. Duty to diagnose
b. Duty to protect

c. Duty to evaluate
d. Duty to treat

Answer: b
Peck v. Counseling Service of Addison County, Inc. was a Vermont Supreme Court case in which John Peck disclosed to his therapist his intent to burn down his parents' barn. The therapist was found negligent because he should have warned the parents of Peck's intent.

What is the standard of proof for civil commitment?

a. More likely than not
b. Preponderance of the evidence
c. Clear and convincing evidence
d. Beyond a reasonable doubt

Answer: c
Addington v. Texas established the standard of proof in civil commitment to a mental hospital as clear and convincing evidence.

Lessard v. Schmidt was decided in which court of law?

a. United States Supreme Court
b. Appellate court
c. Trial court
d. Federal court

Answer: c
Lessard v. Schmidt was a trial court decision regarding civil commitment. The holding affirmed that due process requires safeguards for civil commitment that include the following:

- Right to trial by jury
- No hearsay evidence
- Privilege to remain silent
- Standard of proof
- Notice
- Right to an attorney

What important concept was presented by Judge Bazelon in the case of *Lake v. Cameron*?

a. Least restrictive alternative for treatment
b. Right to refuse treatment

  c. Importance of informed consent
  d. Criminalization of civil commitment

Answer: a

Lake v. Cameron was a Washington, D.C. Court of Appeals case in which an elderly and senile bag lady was civilly committed to St. Elizabeth's Hospital. Judge Bazelon in hearing this case introduced the concept of a least restrictive alternative for treatment.

Which case recognized the patient's right to individualized treatment plans?

  a. *Vacco v. Quill*
  b. *Rogers v. Commissioner*
  c. *Rouse v. Cameron*
  d. *Cruzan v. Director, Missouri DMH*

Answer: c

Rouse v. Cameron was a case where Charles Rouse was involuntarily committed to St. Elizabeth's Hospital in Washington, D.C. and complained that he was not receiving psychiatric treatment there. He filed a habeas corpus that was denied, but the D.C. Court of Appeals, via Judge Bazelon, did recognize the right to treatment for the first time and also emphasized the importance of individualized treatment plans for psychiatric patients.

What was the standard of proof that was established in the case of *Cruzan v. Director, Missouri DMH*?

  a. Probable cause
  b. Preponderance of the evidence
  c. Clear and convincing evidence
  d. Beyond a reasonable doubt

Answer: c

Clear and convincing evidence was the standard of proof in this case involving treatment refusal and the right to die.

Which of the following was not a finding of the court in the case of *Rennie v. Klein*?

  a. Patients must provide written informed consent
  b. Forced medications are acceptable at the discretion of doctors
  c. Advocates in the form of legal counsel must be made available to patients refusing treatment
  d. Forced medications are acceptable in emergency situations

Answer: b

Rennie v. Klein was a case involving the right to refuse treatment. Due to understaffing at a hospital, doctors were not providing informed consent for the administration of psychotropic medications. After hearing this case, the court mandated the following: (1) patients must provide written informed consent, (2) advocates in the form of legal counsel must be made available to patients refusing treatment, (3) forced medications are acceptable in emergency situations, and (4) an informal review by an independent psychiatrist must occur before forcing any medication on a patient.

What was the defining issue in the case of *Burlington Industries v. Ellerth*?

    a. Conduct
    b. Damages
    c. Intent
    d. Restitution

Answer: a
In this case of sexual harassment, the court held that employers are liable for unwelcome and threatening sexual advances made by supervisors even if the threat is not carried out and if the employee suffers no adverse effect. The conduct not the damage is the defining issue.

Which United States Supreme Court case was the first to address sexual harassment as a cause of action?

    a. *Oncale v. Sundowners Offshore Services*
    b. *Gebser v. Lago Vista Independent School District*
    c. *Harris v. Forklift Systems, Inc.*
    d. *Meritor Savings Bank v. Vinson*

Answer: d
Although all of the above cases address sexual harassment, the first United States Supreme Court case to address sexual harassment as a cause of action was *Meritor Savings Bank v. Vinson*. In this case, Michelle Vinson was hired by Meritor and rose through the ranks although she was subjected to dozens of sexual encounters by her supervisor over the course of four years which included fondling, indecent exposure, and rape. She was eventually fired for sick leave and Vinson then sued under a Title VII based on "constant harassment" by her boss. She explained that she had never complained before for fear of losing her job. The court held that hostile environment claims are actionable under Title VII, but the conduct must be severe. The ultimate test was whether the advances were unwelcome.

Which Amendment right was in question in the case of *Vacco v. Quill*?

  a. First
  b. Sixth
  c. Eighth
  d. Fourteenth

Answer: d

Vacco v. Quill dealt with the right to physician-assisted suicide (PAS). The court held that a New York statute banning PAS did not violate the equal protection clause of the Fourteenth Amendment.

Vermont Law 114 was found to violate what Act in the case of *Hargrave v. Vermont*?

  a. Americans with Disabilities Act
  b. Patriot Act
  c. Affordable Care Act
  d. Social Security Act

Answer: a

Hargrave v. Vermont was a 2nd Circuit Court of Appeals case in which Nancy Hargrave, a woman with schizophrenia, had signed a power of attorney (POA) asserting her refusal of electroconvulsive therapy or psychotropic medications. Vermont Law 114 allowed a petition for forced medications. The issue at court was whether VT Law 114 violated the Americans with Disabilities Act (ADA) and the court held that it did. The ADA prohibits discrimination against the mentally ill who have refused treatment via a POA.

In the case of *Pennsylvania Department of Corrections v. Yeskey*, what medical condition precluded Yeskey from participating in boot camp?

  a. Asthma
  b. Hypertension
  c. Diabetes
  d. Obesity

Answer: b

In the case of *Pennsylvania Department of Corrections v. Yeskey*, Ronald Yeskey was held out of boot camp participation, which might have led to an early prison release. The reasoning was his hypertension. The Court found that the American with Disabilities Act (ADA) applies to inmates in state prisons and held that they can sue if excluded from special programs based on their disability.

What major life activity was the issue in the case of *Bragdon v. Abbott*?

  a. Breathing
  b. Toileting
  c. Eating
  d. Reproducing

Answer: d
Ms. Abbott was told by her dentist that due to her HIV-positive status, she would need to have her cavity filled in the hospital, where she would be responsible for the cost. The court held that HIV is protected under the Americans with Disabilities Act because it could influence the major life activity of reproducing.

What United States Supreme Court case held that a contagious disease is a physical impairment?

  a. *Bragdon v. Abbott*
  b. *Sutton v. United Airlines, Inc.*
  c. *School Board of Nassau County Florida v. Arline*
  d. *Toyota Manufacturing Company v. Williams*

Answer: c
In the case of *School Board of Nassau County Florida v. Arline*, the Court held that employers cannot discriminate against disability. The court agreed that Ms. Arline's tuberculosis, which was the impetus for her getting fired from teaching, was a physical impairment leading to disability. This ruling laid the foundation for protection of HIV-positive patients.

What Amendment right was violated in the case of *Graham v. Florida*?

  a. First
  b. Sixth
  c. Eighth
  d. Fourteenth

Answer: c
Sixteen-year-old Terence Graham was sentenced to life in prison without parole for a nonhomicide crime. This was a violation of his Eighth Amendment right. Based on the case of *Roper v. Simmons*, juveniles are less culpable than adults.

The case of *Fare v. Michael C.* dealt with what juvenile right?

  a. Right to refuse treatment
  b. Miranda rights

c. Right to testify
d. Right to treatment

Answer: b
Michael C. was a 16-year-old who was questioned by police officers about a murder. The police gave Michael a Miranda warning and Michael asked for his probation officer but the police refused. They went on to obtain incriminating evidence from Michael. The Court held that the standard for juveniles to waive Miranda was the same as adults (i.e., knowing, intelligent, and voluntary).

Which Amendment right was in question in the case of *McKeiver v. Pennsylvania*?

a. First
b. Sixth
c. Eighth
d. Fourteenth

Answer: d
Joseph McKeiver, 16 years old, was charged with robbery, larceny, and receiving stolen goods valuing 25 cents. His attorney requested a jury trial, which was denied. The Court held that the due process clause of the Fourteenth Amendment did not necessitate a jury trial in juvenile court.

What is the standard established by the United States Supreme Court (USSC) for all delinquency adjudication?

a. Reason to believe
b. Preponderance of the evidence
c. Clear and convincing evidence
d. Beyond a reasonable doubt

Answer: d
In re Winship was a case about a juvenile in the criminal court system. In this case, Samuel Winship was 12 years old when he stole $112 from a purse and was committed to a training school. The USSC determined that the standard for all delinquency adjudication be beyond a reasonable doubt.

All of the following are "Determinative Factors" in deciding a judicial waiver (i.e., trying a juvenile as an adult in court) except:

a. Minor offense
b. Personal circumstances

    c. Public safety
    d. Likelihood of rehabilitation

Answer: a

Kent v. U.S. was the first United States Supreme Court case involving a judicial waiver in juvenile court proceedings. Several "determinative factors" were established including:

- Seriousness/violence of offense
- Offense against person/property
- Probable cause
- Desirability of trying the case in only one court
- Juvenile's personal circumstances
- Prior criminal record
- Public safety
- Likelihood of rehabilitation

Which case determined that a state law requiring two-parent notification of a minor's intent to have an abortion was unconstitutional?

    a. *Planned Parenthood v. Danforth*
    b. *H.L. v. Matheson*
    c. *Carey v. Population Services International*
    d. *Hodgson v. Minnesota*

Answer: d

The outcome of *Hodgson v. Minnesota* was that Minnesota's law requiring two-parent notification prior to a minor's abortion was unconstitutional. This was based on the fact that there was no judicial bypass procedure for mature minors.

    Planned Parenthood v. Danforth struck down a statute stating that women under 18 years old needed to get parental consent prior to an abortion. The Court opined that such women could have an abortion without parental consent so long as the woman had sufficient maturity and understanding.

    In *H.L. v. Matheson* the United States Supreme Court upheld a Utah law stating that doctors must give notice, when possible, to parents when performing an abortion on a minor.

    The Court struck down a statute that prohibited contraception for women under 16 years old in *Carey v. Population Services International*. The Court held that contraception must be available to minors.

What special group was granted authority to admit minors to a psychiatric hospital in the case of *Parham v. J.L. and J.R.?*

    a. Parents
    b. Teachers

c. Police officers
d. Firefighters

Answer: a
The Court upheld parental authority to psychiatrically admit children with a concurring psychiatric opinion and a periodic review of the case.

What was the basis for the court's decision in the case of *Painter v. Bannister*?

a. Preponderance of the evidence
b. Clear and convincing evidence
c. Beyond a reasonable doubt
d. Best interest of the child

Answer: d
This case was heard in the Supreme Court of Iowa. Mr. Painter's wife was killed in a car crash and the widow asked the grandparents of his 7-year-old son to look after the child while he grieved. After one year, Mr. Painter remarried and decided that he wanted his son back but the grandparents refused. Iowa looked at the "best interest of the child" when deciding this case, and they ultimately ruled that what is best for the child is what he needs and not what the parent wants.

Which Amendment right was at issue in the case of *Maryland v. Craig*?

a. First
b. Sixth
c. Eighth
d. Fourteenth

Answer: b
Maryland v. Craig involved the Sixth Amendment right to confront one's accuser. In this case, it was a 6-year-old child who had accused Mr. Craig of sexual assault. The child testified via a one-way closed circuit television because the state argued that testifying in front of Craig would be too distressing for the child. Craig's counsel argued that this violated his Sixth Amendment right to face his accuser. The Court ruled that it is OK to excuse a child from court if the state could make an "adequate showing of necessity," which includes hearing the evidence, finding that the child is traumatized, and that the emotional distress of the child is more than simply "nervousness, excitement, or reluctance."

What was the standard for termination of parental rights in the case of *Santosky v. Kramer*?

a. Preponderance of the evidence
b. Clear and convincing evidence

c. Beyond a reasonable doubt
d. Best interest of the child

Answer: b
Santosky v. Kramer established the standard for termination of parental rights as clear and convincing evidence.

In the case of *Lunderos v. Flood*, doctors are expected to be able to diagnose what in children?

a. Seizure
b. Child abuse
c. Meningitis
d. Cancer

Answer: b
In this California Supreme Court case, the Court established that doctors are expected to make a diagnosis of child abuse. In this particular case, Dr. Flood did not x-ray the skull of an 11-month-old girl with obvious skull fractures and multiple bruises.

In the case of *Hoffman v. Harris*, who was sued?

a. Doctors
b. Hospital administration
c. Nurses
d. Social workers

Answer: d
In this 6th Circuit Court of Appeals case, Mr. Hoffman sued a social worker for reporting him as a suspected child abuser. The social worker was acting on allegations made by the mother of a minor, the latter of whom was the patient. In this case the court held that when it comes to mandatory reporting of child abuse, the social worker enjoys "absolute immunity from liability."

What man was the catalyst for the Sexual Predator Law in Washington?

a. Earl Shriner
b. Adam Walsh
c. Jesse Timmendequas
d. Jacob Wetterling

Answer: a
In 1989 Earl Shriner raped and strangled a 7-year-old boy, cut off his penis, and left him in the woods to die. This happened two years after Shriner

had served a 10-year prison sentence for kidnap and assault of two teenage girls. In reaction to this, Washington State passed the Sexual Predator Law.

Which Amendment right was in question in the case of *Washington v. Glucksberg*?

  a. First
  b. Sixth
  c. Eighth
  d. Fourteenth

Answer: d
Washington v. Glucksberg dealt with the right to physician-assisted suicide (PAS). The state of Washington prohibited PAS and the court found that the ban did not violate the due process clause of the Fourteenth Amendment.

Which Amendment is most commonly challenged in Megan's Law?

  a. First
  b. Fifth
  c. Eighth
  d. Fourteenth

Answer: d
Megan's Law, which was adopted federally, mandates community notification of sex offenders living in a neighborhood. This occurred after 7-year-old Megan Kanka was killed by her neighbor, who unknown to others was a two-time sex offender. Some unintended and unfortunate results of sex offender notification laws include vigilantism, failure of offenders to register, failure of sex offenders to find any housing, and increased risk of relapse due to stress.

Which Amendment right was challenged in the case of *Allen v. Illinois*?

  a. Fourth
  b. Fifth
  c. Eighth
  d. Fourteenth

Answer: b
Terry Allen protested his Fifth Amendment right against self-incrimination was being violated. He had been charged with unlawful restraint and deviant sexual assault. He was never tried and instead the state petitioned to have Allen declared a sexually dangerous person under the Illinois Sexually Dangerous Person Act. Allen had been diagnosed with

psychosis. The Court upheld his detention under the Act because the aim of the state was treatment and not punishment. Ultimately, this was a civil and not criminal issue. Therefore, protection against self-incrimination would not apply.

Which Amendment right was violated in the case of *Specht v. Patterson*?

a. Fourth
b. Sixth
c. Eighth
d. Fourteenth

Answer: d
The Court held that Francis Specht's Fourteenth Amendment right to due process was violated because he was not granted the following protections: right to be present with counsel, notice, hearing, confrontation of the evidence against him, cross-examination of witnesses, and opportunity to offer his own evidence.

Which Amendment right was challenged in the case of *McKune v. Lile*?

a. Fifth
b. Sixth
c. Eighth
d. Fourteenth

Answer: a
Lile argued that his Fifth Amendment right against self-incrimination was violated. Robert Lile was a convicted sex offender and offered some luxuries in prison (i.e., visitors, commissary, minimum security) if he signed an "admission of responsibility" as part of a SATP (Sexual Abuse Treatment Program). He refused to sign. The Court upheld that the SATP serves a vital penological purpose and therefore did not violate Lile's rights.

In the case of *Kansas v. Crane*, what was the diagnosis given to Michael Crane?

a. Schizophrenia
b. Bipolar
c. Exhibitionism
d. Impulse control disorder

Answer: c
Michael Crane argued that his diagnosis of exhibitionism did not qualify as a volitional disorder, and therefore, he should not be convicted as a sexually violent predator.

What was the issue considered in the case of *Frendak v. U.S.*?

 a. Competency
 b. Criminal responsibility
 c. Amnestic disorders
 d. Truancy

Answer: b
Frendak v. U.S. was a D.C. Court of Appeals case involving criminal responsibility. Paula Frendak had murdered her coworker and was found competent to stand trial. The court tried to impose the insanity defense on her. The Court of Appeals held that a trial judge cannot force the insanity defense on a defendant.

The case of *Foucha v. Louisiana* established that persons adjudicated insane cannot be held in psychiatric institutions unless they are found mentally ill and what else?

 a. Incompetent
 b. Noncompliant
 c. Dangerous
 d. Isolated

Answer: c
Foucha v. Louisiana established that persons adjudicated insane could not be held unless found to be both mentally ill and dangerous. Otherwise, detention is a violation of their due process and equal protection. Polysubstance abuse and personality disorders did not qualify as a mental illness.

Which of the following is the Dusky Standard for competency to stand trial?

 a. A defendant has the sufficient present ability to consult with a lawyer and have a rational and factual understanding of the case
 b. A defendant had the sufficient ability to consult with a lawyer and have a rational and factual understanding of the case at the time of the crime
 c. A defendant has the sufficient present ability to consult with their doctor and have a rational and factual understanding of their illness
 d. A defendant has some ability to consult with a lawyer and have a rational and factual understanding of the case

Answer: a

The Dusky Standard states that to be competent to stand trial a defendant has to have the sufficient present ability to consult with a lawyer and a rational and factual understanding of the case.

Which of the following cases did not deal with hypnotically refreshed memories?

   a. *Rock v. Arkansas*
   b. *People v. Shirley*
   c. *Riggins v. Nevada*
   d. *State v. Hurd*

Answer: c
In *Rock v. Arkansas* the Court held that an Arkansas per se rule excluding hypnotically refreshed memories violated the Constitution.

   People v. Shirley was a California Supreme Court case where the court rejected Dr. Orne's safeguards to hypnosis.

   In *State v. Hurd* the Court held that violation of hypnotically refreshed memories was a violation of due process because it could have been used for exoneration.

   Riggins v. Nevada dealt with the issue of forced medications in the criminal context.

Which Amendment right was not in question in the case of *Rock v. Arkansas*?

   a. Fifth
   b. Sixth
   c. Eighth
   d. Fourteenth

Answer: c
In this case, Vickie Rock shot her husband to death. She could not recall the details of the shooting but through hypnosis learned that the gun misfired. She appealed an Arkansas rule that excluded such testimony. The court held that her Fifth, Sixth, and Fourteenth Amendment rights were violated.

Which of the following is not one of Dr. Orne's safeguards to hypnotically refreshed memories?

   a. Hypnotists should be hired by the prosecution
   b. Before hypnosis, the therapist should take a thorough history of the alleged events

   c. Hypnotism sessions should be video-recorded
   d. Only the hypnotist and subject should be present during the session

Answer: a

Dr. Orne's safeguards to hypnosis were established from the case of *State v. Hurd*. They include: (1) licensed psychiatrists should be trained in hypnosis, (2) hypnotists should be independent (i.e., not hired by prosecution or defense), (3) information given to the hypnotist by police should be written, (4) before hypnosis, the therapist should obtain a thorough history of the details of the alleged event, (5) sessions should be video-recorded, and (6) only the therapist and subject should be present during the hypnosis session.

What is a slang phrase for the diminished capacity defense?

   a. "Out of luck defense"
   b. "Drunk as a skunk defense"
   c. "Twinkie defense"
   d. "Win some lose some defense"

Answer: c

After Dan White killed Mayor Moscone and Supervisor Harvey Milk of San Francisco he argued that high blood sugar from too many sweets drove him to murder. This was a diminished capacity defense that has since been nicknamed the "Twinkie defense."

Which of the following is a sign of impairment from a mental condition according to the Social Security Act (SSA)?

   a. Marked restrictions in life activities of daily living
   b. Limited social functioning
   c. Repeated episodes of decompensation in work only
   d. Oversleeping for work

Answer: a

The SSA offers disability benefits through Social Security Disability Income (SSDI) and through Supplemental Security Income (SSI). For SSA purposes, a disabling psychiatric condition is one that renders an individual unable to engage in work for substantial gain by reason of a mental or physical impairment that has lasted or is expected to last at least 12 months.

   In assessing impairment that may flow from a mental condition, the SSA considers the following:

   • Marked restriction in activities of daily living
   • Marked difficulties in maintaining social functioning

- Deficiencies in concentration, persistence, or pace, resulting in frequent failure to complete tasks in a timely fashion in work settings
- Repeated episodes of deterioration or decompensation in work or work-life settings that cause the individual to withdraw from the situation or to experience an exacerbation of signs and symptoms

In the case of *Montana v. Egelhoff,* excessive intake of what substance was the basis for a diminished capacity defense?

a. Cocaine
b. Sweets
c. Ecstasy
d. Alcohol

Answer: d
Egelhoff killed two people while intoxicated with alcohol. Based on a new Montana law, the jury was instructed to not consider the defendant's intoxication in the mens rea and the United States Supreme Court held that Montana's law upheld the Constitution.

What is an Alford plea?

a. Pleading no contest while protesting innocence
b. Pleading for mercy from the court
c. Entering into a plea bargain while protesting innocence
d. Pleading guilty but asking the court to consider mitigating factors for a reduced sentence

Answer: c
An "Alford plea" is entering into a plea bargain while protesting innocence. When a plea is knowing, intelligent, and voluntary, there is no violation to the Fifth Amendment.

Which of the following is a status crime?

a. Theft
b. Homelessness
c. Assault
d. Murder

Answer: b
In the 1960s people could be arrested for status crimes such as homelessness, vagrancy, and drug addiction. *Robinson v. California* helped to remove status crimes. Prosecution for these was declared a violation of the Eighth Amendment right against cruel and unusual punishment.

What was "Operation Baxstrom"?

a. The transport of sexual offenders from prison cells into solitary confinement
b. The release of a large number of inmates into the community
c. The mass transit of felony offenders to securely locked facilities
d. The permanent closure of long-term psychiatric facilities

Answer: b
"Operation Baxstrom" was the release of a large number of inmates into the community. This resulted from the case *Baxstrom v. Herald* where prisoners argued that their Fourteenth Amendment rights should be upheld.

According to the Jessica Lunsford Act, child molesters in the state of Florida are required to wear what?

a. Orange jumpsuits
b. Scarlet letter
c. GPS tracking device
d. Identification card

Answer: c
After the rape and murder of a 9-year-old girl by a man who was a sex offender but had moved states, the state of Florida enacted the Jessica Lunsford Act. This legislation requires that child molesters in Florida wear a GPS.

In the case of *Riggins v. Nevada*, the United States Supreme Court opined that the state is obligated to establish what when treating prisoners with psychotropic medications?

a. Duty
b. Benefit
c. Alternatives
d. Need

Answer: d
Involuntary medication of pretrial detainees violates the Sixth and Fourteenth Amendments. The state is obligated to establish a need for treatment.

What Amendment right was in question in the case of *Washington v. Harper*?

a. Fourth
b. Fifth

    c. Sixth
    d. Fourteenth

Answer: d
According to the "Turner test," forced medication is okay as long as it "reasonably relates to a legitimate penological interest."

What is the meaning of the "Bell test"?

    a. A pretrial detainee can be subjected to any conditions
    b. A pretrial detainee cannot be subjected to conditions that are disproportionate to their accused crime
    c. A pretrial detainee cannot be subjected to conditions that are not reasonably related to a legitimate government interest
    d. A pretrial detainee cannot be subjected to conditions that could lead to physical or mental deterioration

Answer: c
Bell v. Wolfish addressed the constitutional rights of pretrial detainees. The Court ruled that a pretrial detainee cannot be subjected to conditions that are not reasonably related to a legitimate government interest. This is known as the "Bell test."

What was the issue in the case of *State v. Perry*?

    a. Treatment of a defendant to restore them to competency for trial
    b. Forcibly medicating a defendant pleading not guilty by reason of insanity
    c. Treatment of a prisoner deemed incompetent to be executed
    d. Transfer of a prisoner to a psychiatric institution

Answer: c
State v. Perry was a Louisiana Supreme Court Case that dealt with the psychiatric treatment of a man convicted of murder and sentenced to death. While awaiting execution, Michael Perry became psychotic and was deemed incompetent to be executed. Initially the Department of Corrections said that he could be forcibly medicated to regain competence, but the United States Supreme Court remanded him based on *Washington v. Harper*.

Which Act did President Obama sign into law only five days after taking office?

    a. Affordable Health Care Act
    b. Unlocking Consumer Choice and Wireless Competition Act

c. Lilly Ledbetter Fair Pay Act
d. Veterans Health Care Budget Reform and Transparency Act

Answer: c
The Lilly Ledbetter Fair Pay Act was signed by President Obama on January 29, 2009. This Act amended the Civil Rights Act of 1964 and laxed the statute of limitations to file for pay discrimination and other civil rights employment violations. This was a direct response to the 2007 United States Supreme Court case of *Ledbetter v. Goodyear Tire and Rubber Company.*

What was the issue in the case of *Panetti v. Quarterman*?

a. Competence to stand trial
b. Competence to be executed
c. Competence to provide informed consent
d. Competence to hold a driver's license

Answer: b
Panetti killed his wife's parents in front of his wife and daughter. The Court determined that Panetti knew the facts but didn't have a rational understanding about the execution and therefore was incompetent to be executed.

Which Amendment right was questioned in the case of *Ford v. Wainwright*?

a. First
b. Fourth
c. Sixth
d. Eighth

Answer: d
Alvin Ford was convicted of murder and sentenced to death. He appeared highly insane and it was determined that the Eighth Amendment prohibits the execution of an insane person.

Which United States Supreme Court (USSC) Justice suggested an "execution competency standard"?

a. Justice Powell
b. Justice O'Connor
c. Justice Roberts
d. Justice Scalia

Answer: a

In the case of *Ford v. Wainwright,* Justice Powell suggested an "execution competency standard." This entails the convicted to be aware that an execution is happening and to also know the reason for it. This was as a result of the USSC opinion that the Eighth Amendment prohibits execution of an insane person.

Which Amendment right was in question in the case of *Ring v. Arizona?*

a. First
b. Fourth
c. Sixth
d. Eighth

Answer: c
Ring's Sixth Amendment right to a trial by jury was violated. Ring was charged with robbing an armored van and murdering the driver. He was convicted of a felony murder. When it comes to making the final decision on the death penalty, only a jury can decide this.

What was the issue in the case of *Payne v. Tennessee?*

a. Competence
b. Victim impact statements (VIS)
c. Hearsay
d. Child witness testimony

Answer: b
The United States Supreme Court opined that allowing VIS by the prosecution in court does not violate the defendant's Eighth Amendment rights.

What controversial testimony was provided by Dr. Grigson in the case of *Barefoot v. Estelle?*

a. Hypothetical questions
b. Hearsay evidence
c. Hypnotically refreshed memories
d. Unqualified testimony

Answer: a
Dr. Grigson provided expert testimony in the case of *Barefoot v. Estelle.* His testimony occurred during the criminal sentencing phase. Dr. Grigson had never evaluated Thomas Barefoot who was convicted of murder, but he did testify regarding hypothetical questions. The Court allowed this if questions were related to the risk of future dangerousness.

In the case of *In re Gault*, the United States Supreme Court (USSC) said that in hearings that could potentially lead to the institutionalization of juveniles, they had a right to all of the following except:

a. Notice of charges
b. Trial by jury
c. Legal counsel
d. Privilege against self-incrimination

Answer: b
Gerard Gault, 15 years old, filed a writ of habeas corpus after he was sentenced to six years' incarceration for making crank phone calls while on probation for a minor property offense. This court hearing was referred to as a "kangaroo court" and the USSC declared that in hearings that could potentially lead to the institutionalization of juveniles, they had a right to:

• Notice of charges
• Legal counsel
• Privilege against self-incrimination
• Confrontation of their accuser and cross-examination of witnesses

Which two Amendment rights were questioned in the case of *Estelle v. Smith*?

a. First and Fourth
b. Fourth and Fifth
c. Fifth and Sixth
d. Eighth and Fourteenth

Answer: c
Ernest Smith murdered a store clerk and was sentenced to death. Dr. Grigson had evaluated Smith for competency to stand trial. Later, Dr. Grigson served as a surprise witness and testified about Smith's risk of future dangerousness. Smith claimed this violated his Fifth Amendment right against self-incrimination and Sixth Amendment right to have counsel. The Court agreed on both counts.

Which two Amendment rights were questioned in the case of *Roper v. Simmons*?

a. First and Fourth
b. Fourth and Fifth
c. Fifth and Sixth
d. Eighth and Fourteenth

Answer: d

Roper v. Simmons involved juveniles and the death penalty. The state of Missouri sought to execute 17-year-old Christopher Simmons who murdered Shirley Cook. The Court held that the death penalty for juveniles violated the Eighth and Fourteenth Amendments.

Which United States Supreme Court Justice suggested an "evolving standard of decency" with regard to the death penalty and mental retardation?

    a. Justice Powell
    b. Justice O'Connor
    c. Justice Roberts
    d. Justice Scalia

Answer: b
In ruling on the case of *Penry v. Lynaugh,* Justice O'Connor noted that at this time there was an "evolving standard of decency … but no evidence of a consensus yet."

In 2002, what was the evidence that Americans did not support the death penalty of individuals with mental retardation?

    a. Best guess
    b. Brief questionnaire
    c. Polling data
    d. AMA directive

Answer: c
Polling data collected from Americans suggested that the majority were not in support of execution of mentally retarded individuals. It was a violation of the Eighth Amendment.

What type of discrimination was the basis for the argument in the case of *McCleskey v. Kemp*?

    a. Racial
    b. Sexual
    c. Age
    d. Disability

Answer: a
McCleskey was an African American who killed a white police officer and was then sentenced to death. He argued that this was racial discrimination and violated his Eighth and Fourteenth Amendments.

Which Federal Rule of Evidence was cited in the rationale for the Court's decision in the case of *Jaffee v. Redmond*?

    a. 402
    b. 501
    c. 601
    d. 702

Answer: b

Confidential communication between a licensed psychotherapist and her patients in the course of diagnosis and treatment are protected from compelled disclosure under Rule 501 of the Federal Rules of Evidence. The court ordered that this privilege should extend to communications made to a licensed social worker.

402 Federal Rule of Evidence establishes that evidence that is not relevant is not admissible.

601 Federal Rule of Evidence establishes the framework for competency to testify in general.

702 Federal Rule of Evidence establishes the criteria for testimony by expert witnesses.

There are two exceptions cited in the case *Canterbury v. Spence* as to the physician's responsibility to employ the objective standard and provide patients with informed consent. Which of the following is one of those exceptions?

    a. Full disclosure of risks would undoubtedly cause the patient to reject the treatment recommendation
    b. The physician is an intern and therefore, not yet fully qualified to obtain informed consent
    c. The situation is an emergency
    d. The adverse risk is so rare that it is nearly negligible

Answer: c

The Court identifies two exceptions to the duty to disclose:

- Emergency situation
- Disclosure of the risk is medically contraindicated because the disclosure itself may do psychological harm or complicate the treatment

What is the protection guaranteed under the First Amendment?

    a. Freedom of speech
    b. Freedom from unreasonable search and seizure

   c. Proscription of cruel and unusual punishment
   d. Right to due process

Answer: a
The First Amendment guarantees the right to freedom of speech. This is a right that is even retained by involuntarily institutionalized persons

   The Fourth Amendment provides freedom from unreasonable search and seizure.

   The Eighth Amendment proscribes cruel and unusual punishment.
   The Fourteenth Amendment provides the right to due process.

In the case of *Jablonski v. U.S.*, which was not one of the malpractice claims raised against Dr. Kopiloff (the doctor who failed to hospitalize the very dangerous Jablonski)?

   a. Failure to protect
   b. Failure to get past medical records
   c. Failure to warn
   d. Failure to give antipsychotics

Answer: d
Mr. Jablonski killed his wife's mother. Mrs. Jablonski filed a wrongful death claim and asserted the death was the result of malpractice by the Veterans Administration doctors because of:

   • Failure to protect
   • Failure to get past medical records
   • Failure to warn Ms. Kimball

What was the legal issue in the case of *Naidu v. Laird*?

   a. Confidentiality and privilege
   b. Informed consent
   c. Duty to protect
   d. Expert testimony

Answer: c
In this case, a doctor failed to protect a third party from foreseeable harm by a psychotic man. Dr. Naidu discharged a psychotic patient from the hospital on the basis of the patient being committed voluntarily, requesting to leave, and having undergone a lengthy admission. The Supreme Court of Delaware concluded that Putney's desire to leave the hospital in no way obligated the doctor to release him when he posed a real threat to a third party.

What is the name of the test that considers "admissibility of scientific evidence based on general acceptance of the methodology by the scientific community"?

   a. Daubert test
   b. Reliability test
   c. Joiner test
   d. Frye test

Answer: d
The Frye test came out of the need for a court to determine what qualifies as admissible expert testimony and states the "admissibility of scientific evidence based on general acceptance of the methodology by the scientific community."

What qualifies as being in the "zone of danger" for psychic injury claims?

   a. Not being harmed but being personally endangered by an act
   b. Being physically harmed but not as severely as others by an act
   c. Witnessing from afar an act but having no threat to your body
   d. Hearing about a significant event that leads to emotional harm

Answer: a
The "zone of danger" refers to an act that renders an individual physically unharmed but personally endangered by that act. An example of this is found in the case of *Dillon v. Legg*, where a girl is nearly hit by the car that kills her sister.

What is the test for sexual harassment, as the court ruled in *Meritor Savings Bank v. Vinson*?

   a. Involuntary participation in sex acts
   b. Unwelcome sexual advancements
   c. Feeling physically threatened
   d. Constant ridicule and insult

Answer: b
The test for sexual harassment is simply if advancements made are unwelcome.

Under which Title did Vinson file suit against Meritor Savings Bank for the constant harassment by her boss?

   a. Title V
   b. Title VII

c. Title VIII
d. Title X

Answer: b
Title VII affords employees the right to work in an environment free from discriminatory intimidation, ridicule, and insult.

Why was Dr. Hartogs found guilty of medical malpractice in the case of *Roy v. Hartogs*?

a. Improper prescribing
b. Failing to provide informed consent
c. Inadequate documentation
d. Sex with his patient

Answer: d
Dr. Hartogs had convinced his patient that sexual intercourse should be part of her therapy. She later suffered emotional distress and required psychiatric admissions. The court agreed that Dr. Hartogs had committed medical malpractice and awarded monetary damages to Roy.

What was the basis for the court's original determination that Milton Dusky was competent to stand trial?

a. Ability to assist in his own defense
b. Orientation
c. Rational and factual understanding of the case
d. Full knowledge of courtroom procedures

Answer: b
This decision was ultimately overturned by the United States Supreme Court who held that a finding of orientation was not a fair competency test. The court held that "the test must be whether [the defendant] has sufficient present ability to consult with his lawyer with a reasonable degree of rational understanding—and whether he has a rational as well as factual understanding of the proceedings against him."

When a court is considering whether or not amnesia precludes a defendant from being competent to stand trial, as in the case of *Wilson v. U.S.*, which of the following is not a factor that the court should consider?

a. Extent to which amnesia affected the defendant's ability to consult with a lawyer
b. Extent to which amnesia affected the defendant's ability to testify on their behalf

  c. Extent to which the government could assist the defendant and counsel in reconstruction of the event
  d. Strength of the defense's case

Answer: d
The court found that Mr. Wilson was competent to stand trial after considering a number of factors important to amnesia and competence to stand trial. All of the above are considerations for the court except for d. It is the strength of the prosecutor's case, not the defense that must be considered by the court.

Leroy Hendricks was confined in Kansas beyond his prison sentence for sexual offenses due to his mental disorder and high likelihood of recidivism of predatory sexual acts. He challenged his confinement on the basis of all of the following except which?

  a. Substantive due process
  b. Double jeopardy
  c. Right to confront accuser
  d. Ex post facto

Answer: c
Kansas enacted the Sexually Violent Predator Act. This legislation established a procedure for civil commitment of inmates after their prison sentence provided that they have a mental disorder or personality disorder and were likely to engage in predatory sexual acts if released into the community.

In the case of *Colorado v. Connelly*, Chief Justice Rehnquist wrote for the majority of the United States Supreme Court and restricted the concept of voluntary confession to mean only that the confession was made without all of the following except:

  a. Intimidation
  b. Coercion
  c. Encouragement
  d. Deception

Answer: c
Rehnquist restricted the concept of voluntary confession to mean only that the confession was made without intimidation, coercion, or deception.

What standard for competency to stand trial was established by the case of *Cooper v. Oklahoma*?

  a. Best guess
  b. Preponderance of the evidence

    c. Clear and convincing evidence
    d. Beyond a reasonable doubt

Answer: b
Oklahoma's prior statute held that defendants were competent unless proven otherwise by clear and convincing evidence. This was overturned because Oklahoma's law had allowed the state to try a defendant who was more likely than not to be incompetent. This was a violation of the Fourteenth Amendment.

What is the test for insanity in a criminal case?

    a. Dusky Standard
    b. M'Naghten's Rule
    c. Reasonable Person
    d. Strict Scrutiny

Answer: b
According to M'Naghten's Rule, for a defendant to be found insane, "It must be clearly provided that, at the time of the committing of the act, the party accused was laboring under such a defect of reason, from disease of the mind, as not to know the nature and quality of the act he was doing; or, if he did know it, that he did not know he was doing what was wrong."

What are the requirements to hold an insanity acquittee in a psychiatric hospital according to the holding in *Foucha v. Louisiana*?

    a. Mentally ill and dangerous
    b. Mentally ill and disabled
    c. Mentally ill and amnestic
    d. Mentally ill and refusing treatment

Answer: a
Insanity acquittees cannot be held in psychiatric hospitals unless deemed to be mentally ill and dangerous.

Which of the following is not an actuarial risk assessment for violence?

    a. HCR-20
    b. TOMM
    c. VRAG
    d. Psychopathy checklist

Answer: b
The TOMM is the Test of Memory Malingering. The other tests assess violence.

When was the first execution of a juvenile offender?

a. 1642
b. 1742
c. 1842
d. 1942

Answer: a

Thomas Granger was the first juvenile to be executed in 1642 in Plymouth Colony after he was convicted of bestiality for sodomizing a horse. The United States Supreme Court declared that the death penalty of a juvenile was unconstitutional in the case of *Roper v. Simmons*.

What Amendment rights did Vickie Rock argue were taken from her when an Arkansas court refused to allow testimony of her hypnotically refreshed memories?

a. First, Fourth, Fifth
b. Fourth, Fifth, Sixth
c. Fifth, Sixth, Fourteenth
d. Sixth, Eighth, Fourteenth

Answer: c

Arkansas' ruling that excluded Rock's hypnotically refreshed testimony violated the following Constitutional rights:

- Fifth Amendment rights—Every defendant can testify on their own behalf
- Sixth Amendment rights—Defendants can call witnesses on their behalf
- Fourteenth Amendment rights—Due process includes a right to offer testimony

In the case of *Atkins v. Virginia*, which Amendment right was challenged in the sentencing of the mentally retarded man, Daryl Atkins, to death by execution?

a. Fourth
b. Sixth
c. Eighth
d. Fourteenth

Answer: c

In this 2002 case, the court held that standards of decency had evolved and the execution of the mentally retarded would be equal to cruel and unusual punishment. By the time this case was heard, there was new polling data from Americans that reflected the opinion above.

In the case of *Roper v. Simmons*, the United States Supreme Court opined that execution of a minor violated which Amendments?

  a. Fourth and Eighth
  b. Sixth and Eighth
  c. Sixth and Fourteenth
  d. Eighth and Fourteenth

Answer: d
This case was decided in 2005, at which time there was a maturing society and likewise, an evolving standard of decency. The court held that just like execution of the mentally retarded was a violation of the Eighth and Fourteenth Amendments, so was execution of a minor.

What was the Louisiana Supreme Court's opinion regarding medicating a person with the purpose to achieve competence for execution?

  a. They were in favor when the crime was so heinous that it served a legitimate government interest
  b. They were in favor when victim impact statements compelled a jury to rule in favor of medication to achieve competence for execution
  c. They were against this as a matter of the Constitution
  d. They were against as a matter of expense and financial burden to the state

Answer: c
The Louisiana Supreme Court heard the case of *State v. Perry* and in 1992 held that Michael Perry, who was convicted of five murders, should not be forcibly medicated to gain competence for execution. The Court affirmed Perry's incompetence and ruled the following:

  • A prisoner cannot be medicated against his will
  • Medicating someone against their will for the purpose of making them competent to be executed was cruel and unusual punishment
  • Such actions violated the Louisiana right to privacy guaranteed in the state's constitution

Which case is the origin for informed consent?

  a. *Salgo v. Leland Stanford Junior University Board of Trustees*
  b. *Natanson v. Kline*

c. *Canterbury v. Spence*
d. *Schloendorff v. Society of New York Hospital*

Answer: d
Although all of the above cases deal with informed consent, it was *Schloendorff v. Society of New York Hospital*, a 1914 case that is the origin of informed consent. Judge Cardoza said in this case that "Every human being of adult years and sound mind has a right to determine what shall be done with his body and a surgeon who operates without consent performs assault and is liable for damages."

In the case of *Ford v. Wainwright*, which Justice suggested an execution competency standard?

a. Justice Rehnquist
b. Justice Powell
c. Justice O'Connor
d. Justice Scalia

Answer: b
Justice Powell suggested this execution competency standard:

- Offender must be aware of what's happening
- Offender must know the reason for what's happening

The Wetterling Act imposes stringent registration programs for sex offenders. This includes that in all states sex offenders must register for how many years?

a. 5
b. 10
c. 15
d. 20

Answer: b
The Wetterling Act was enacted after 11-year-old Jacob Wetterling was killed by a man who had been staying at a halfway house after release from prison. Unknown to the community was the fact that the halfway house was specifically housing sex offenders.

What are the two mens rea for reckless behaviors that qualify under deliberate indifference?

a. Subjective and objective recklessness
b. Retrospective and prospective recklessness

c. Inherent and obvious recklessness
d. Criminal and procedural recklessness

Answer: a
Subjective recklessness is when a person knows about risk and disregards it.

Objective recklessness is when the risk of harm to a person is so high that one should have known.

What is the meaning of the "standard of care" for physicians?

a. The physician is required to possess and exercise that reasonable skill and knowledge ordinarily possessed and exercised by other members of his profession in all circumstances.
b. The physician is required to possess and exercise that reasonable skill and knowledge ordinarily possessed and exercised by other members of his profession in similar circumstances.
c. The physician is required to possess and exercise that reasonable skill and knowledge always possessed and exercised by elite members of his profession in similar circumstances.
d. The physician is required to possess and exercise that perfect skill and knowledge always possessed and exercised by other members of his profession in similar circumstances.

Answer: b
The physician is required to possess and exercise that reasonable skill and knowledge ordinarily possessed and exercised by other members of his profession in similar circumstances. Medical malpractice occurs when there is a dereliction of duty that directly leads to damages.

By what standard must the state prove its case before there is a finding of permanent neglect so that parental rights are terminated?

a. Parental rights can never be fully terminated
b. Preponderance of the evidence
c. Clear and convincing evidence
d. Beyond a reasonable doubt

Answer: c
The standard for termination of parental rights was determined in the case of *Santosky v. Kramer.* The court decided that a standard of preponderance of the evidence was not fair and would deprive natural parents of due process.

What does SORNA stand for?

a. Serial Offender Registry and Notification Act
b. Sexual Offender Registry and Notification Act
c. Substance Offender Registry and Notification Act
d. Serious Offender Registry and Notification Act

Answer: b

SORNA is the Sexual Offender Registry and Notification Act, which expanded the sex offender policy by enhancing penalty for crimes against children. It includes the following points: (1) prisoners must register prior to release from prison, (2) it is retroactive, (3) it requires registration in multiple states if necessary, and (4) it established a juvenile sex offender registry.

Fifteen-year-old Gerald Gault argued that what was violated when he was taken into custody for making crank phone calls and sentenced to the State Industrial School for six years?

a. Right to freedom of speech
b. Right to be silent
c. Right against self-incrimination
d. Right to due process

Answer: d

In 1964, Gault was taken into custody. He filed a writ of habeas corpus arguing that the Arizona juvenile code violated his due process rights by:

• Not requiring that parents and children be apprised of the specific charges
• Not requiring proper notice of a hearing
• Not providing for an appeal
• Allowing the use by juvenile court of unsworn hearsay testimony
• The failure to make a record of the proceedings

What was 16-year-old Terence Graham's sentence after being convicted of attempted robbery in Florida?

a. Life in prison
b. 1 year in prison
c. 5 years in prison
d. 10 years in prison

Answer: a

Terence Graham contested his sentence to life in prison without parole in the case of *Graham v. Florida.* The court held that Graham's sentence violated the Eighth Amendment. (It had already been decided based in *Roper v. Simmons* that juveniles are considered less culpable than adults.)

What were the requests of the Sexual Abuse Treatment Program (SATP) that was offered to Robert Lile while in prison for a sex offense?

    a. Admission of responsibility
    b. Hormonal treatment
    c. Disclosure of partners in crime
    d. Psychiatric admission

Answer: a
The SATP required an "admission of responsibility" whereby Lile would be required to tell authorities of other crimes committed and take a polygraph test. If an offender refused to participate in the SATP then they would be subjected to a transfer to maximum security, lose visitation, and also lose access to commissary.

Which Act did Graydon Comstock argue was unconstitutional in that it contributed to his indefinite detention in prison?

    a. Jessica Lunsford Act
    b. Wetterling Act
    c. Kanka Act
    d. Adam Walsh Act

Answer: d
The Adam Walsh Child Protection Act of 2006 expanded sex offender policies by enhancing penalties for those who sexually exploited children, expanding Internet investigations and prosecution for child pornography, and, most important, adding a central compilation of all state sex offender registries into one uniform national sex offender registry.

Which Amendment right was in question in the case of *Specht v. Patterson*?

    a. Fifth
    b. Sixth
    c. Eighth
    d. Fourteenth

Answer: d
Under the Sex Offender Act of Colorado, a person convicted of a sex crime represented a "threat of bodily harm" to the public or was a mentally ill habitual offender. The procedure for making this determination was found to violate the Fourteenth Amendment. It relied only on a psychiatric

examination and written report recommending whether or not the defendant was treatable as a sex offender.

Considering the case of *Kansas v. Hendricks*, what was the diagnosis of Leroy Hendricks?

   a. Antisocial personality
   b. Impulse control disorder
   c. Psychosis
   d. Pedophilia

Answer: d
Hendricks used that diagnosis to argue the fact that he did not qualify for civil commitment after completing his prison sentence for the sexual abuse of children. The Act provided civil commitment for persons found to have a mental abnormality or personality disorder. The United States Supreme Court opined that pedophilia did in fact qualify as a mental disorder. Hendricks also challenged his commitment based on three other issues: substantive due process, double jeopardy, and ex post facto. The Court rejected Hendricks's arguments on all counts.

Who passed the Prison Rape Elimination Act?

   a. Ronald Reagan
   b. Bill Clinton
   c. George W. Bush
   d. Barack Obama

Answer: c
President Bush signed the Act into law on September 4, 2003.

Operation Baxstrom, the release of a large number of civilly committed patients into the community, was the direct result of Johnnie Baxstrom's unfair civil commitment following the end of his penal sentence. His commitment was unfair because it violated which Amendment right?

   a. Fifth
   b. Sixth
   c. Seventh
   d. Fourteenth

Answer: d
It violated the equal protection clause of the Fourteenth Amendment in two respects:

   • All nonprisoners facing civil commitment have the right to a full jury trial to determine whether they are mentally ill

- No other person may be committed to a Department of Corrections facility without a judicial finding that they are too dangerously mentally ill to be treated safely in a civil hospital

Which court decided the case of *Lessard v. Schmidt*?

a. United States Supreme Court
b. District Appeals Court
c. Superior Court
d. Trial Court

Answer: d

In this case, Alberta Lessard was taken from her home in Wisconsin and committed to a psychiatric hospital without notification of the proceedings. Individuals civilly committed to a mental institution in Wisconsin lost numerous civil rights:

- Presumption of competency
- Right to make contracts and sue
- Right to marry
- Right to professional licenses
- Right to drive
- Right to vote
- Right to serve on juries

Committed individuals were far more likely to face tremendous stigma and difficulties returning to life outside of the institution.

In a trial court decision, it was found that Lessard's due process rights were violated and a number of procedural safeguards were cited as constitutional requirements for commitment of the mentally ill:

- Patient must be given timely notice of charges and notice of all rights
- A probable cause hearing must be held within forty-eight hours
- Patient has the right to representation by an attorney
- Hearsay evidence may not be admitted in the hearing
- Patient retains the privilege against self-incrimination and must be informed that any information provided during examination may be used against him or her in the hearing
- State must prove beyond a reasonable doubt that the patient is both mentally ill and dangerous
- State must demonstrate that less restrictive alternatives to commitment are not available or not suitable

Who argued in the *American Bar Association Journal* that treatment serves a quid pro quo justification for hospitalization?

    a. Dr. Morton Brinbaum
    b. Justice O'Connor
    c. Justice Rehnquist
    d. Dr. Benjamin Rush

Answer: a

This argument was considered by the courts in the case of *Donaldson v. O'Connor*. The Circuit Court of Appeals found that a right to treatment exists in the due process clause of the Fourteenth Amendment.

    In this case, the United States Supreme Court granted certiorari but nonetheless chose not to establish a constitutional right to treatment.

What illness was recognized as qualifying for disability in the case of *Bragdon v. Abbott*?

    a. Tuberculosis
    b. Myopia
    c. Spina bifida
    d. HIV

Answer: d

HIV qualifies as a disability which is defined as a physical or mental impairment that substantially limits one or more major life activities of the individual. The reasoning in this case was based on the fact that any illness that impairs a major life function is covered by the Americans with Disabilities Act. Since reproduction is a major life function, and children of HIV-infected women are affected, then it qualifies as a disability.

Legal case references

Addington v. Texas, 441 U.S. 418, 99 S.Ct. 1804 (1979)
Aetna v. McCabe, 556 F. Supp. 1342 (1983)
Ake v. Oklahoma, 470 U.S. 68, 105 S.Ct. 1087 (1985)
Allen v. Illinois, 478 U.S. 364, 106 S.Ct. 2988 (1986)
Atkins v. Virginia, 122 S.Ct. 2242 (2002)
Barefoot v. Estelle, 463 U.S. 880, 103 S.Ct. 3383 (1983)
Baxstrom v. Herold, 383 U.S. 107, 86 S.Ct. 760 (1966)
Bell v. Wolfish, 441 U.S. 520 (1979)
Bellotti v. Baird, 443 U.S. 622 (1979)
Bragdon v. Abbott, 118 S.Ct. 2198 (1998)
Burlington v. Ellerth, 524 U.S. 742 (1998)
Canterbury v. Spence, 150 U.S. App. D.C. 263, 464 F.2d 772 (1972)
Carey v. Population Services International, 431 U.S. 678 (1977)
Carter v. General Motors, 361 Mich. 577, 106 N.W.2d 105 (1960)
Clites v. Iowa, 322 N.W. 2d 917 (Iowa Ct. App. 1982)
Coleman v. Wilson, 912 F.Supp. 1282 (1995)
Colorado v. Connelly, 479 U.S. 157, 107 S.Ct. 515 (1986)
Cooper v. Oklahoma, 116 S.Ct. 1923 (1996)
Corcoran v. United Healthcare, Inc., 965 F.2d 1321 (1992)
Cruzan v. Director, Missouri DMH, 497 U.S. 261, 110 S.Ct. 2841 (1990)
Daubert v. Merrell Dow, 61 U.S.L.W. 4805, 113 S.Ct. 2786 (1993)
DeShaney v. Winnebago, 489 U.S. 189, 109 S.Ct. 998 (1989)
Dillon v. Legg, 69 Cal. Rptr. 72, 441 P.2d 912 (1968)
Doe v. Roe, 400 N.Y. Supp.2d 668 (1977)
Donaldson v. O'Connor, 493 U.S. F.2d 507 (5th Cir., 1974)
Drope v. Missouri, 420 U.S. 162, 95 S.Ct. 896 (1975)
Dukes v. U.S. Healthcare, Inc., 57 F.3d 350 (3rd Cir. 1995)
Durham v. U.S., 94 U.S. App. D.C. 228, 214 F.2d 862 (1954)
Dusky v. U.S., 362 U.S. 402, 80 S.Ct. 788 (1960)
Estelle v. Gamble, 429 U.S. 97, 97 S.Ct. 285 (1976)
Estelle v. Smith, 451 U.S. 454, 101 S.Ct. 1866 (1981)
Fare v. Michael C., 442 U.S. 707 (1979)
Farmer v. Brennan, 114 S.Ct. 1970 (1994)
Ford v. Wainwright, 477 U.S. 399, 106 S.Ct. 2595 (1986)
Foucha v. Louisiana, 112 S.Ct. 1780 (1992)
Frendak v. U.S., 408 A.2d 364 (D.C. 1979)
Frye v. U.S., 293 F. 1013 (1923)

Gault, In Re, 387 U.S. 1, 87 S.Ct. 1428 (1967)
Gebser v. Lago Vista Independent School District, 524 U.S. 274 (1998)
General Electric v. Joiner, 118 S.Ct. 512 (1997)
Gerber v. Hickman, 103 F.Supp.2d 1214 (2000)
Godinez v. Moran, 61 U.S.L.W. 4749, 113 S.Ct. 2680 (1993)
Graham v. Florida, 130 S. Ct. 2011 (2010)
H.L. v. Matheson, 450 U.S. 398 (1981)
Hargrave v. Vermont, 340 F. 3d 27 (2003)
Harris v. Forklift Systems, Inc., 114 S.Ct. 367 (1993)
Hodgson v. Minnesota, 497 U.S. 417 (1990)
Hoffman v. Harris, 511 U.S. 1060 (1994)
Ibn-Tamas v. U.S., 407 A.2d 626 (D.C. 1979)
In re Winship, 397 U.S. 358 (1970)
Indiana v. Edwards, 554 U.S. 164 (2008)
Irving Independent School District v. Tatro, 468 U.S. 883, 104 S.Ct. 3371 (1984)
Jablonski v. U.S., 712 F.2d 391 (9th Cir. 1983)
Jackson v. Indiana, 406 U.S. 715, 92 S.Ct. 1845 (1972)
Jaffee v. Redmond, 116 S.Ct. 1923 (1996)
Jones v. U.S., 463 U.S. 354, 103 S.Ct. 3043 (1983)
Kaimowitz v. Michigan DMH, 1 MDLR 147 (1976)
Kansas v. Crane, 534 U.S. 407 (2002)
Kansas v. Hendricks, 117 S.Ct. 2072 (1997)
Kent v. U.S., 383 U.S. 541 (1966)
Kumho Tire Co. v. Carmichael, 119 S.Ct. 1167 (1999)
Lake v. Cameron, 124 U.S. App. D.C. 264, 364 F.2d 657 (1966)
Landeros v. Flood, 17 Cal. 3d 399, 551 P.2d 389 (1976)
Ledbetter v. Goodyear Tire & Rubber Co., 550 U.S. 616 (2007)
Lessard v. Schmidt, 349 F. Supp. 1078 (E.D. Wis. 1972)
Lifschutz, In Re, 2 Cal. 3d 415, 467 P.2d 557 (1970)
Lipari v. Sears, 497 F. Supp. 185 (D. Neb. 1980)
M'Naghten's Case, 8 Eng. Rep. 718, 8 Eng. Rep. 722 (1843)
Maryland v. Craig, 497 U.S. 836 (1990)
McCleskey v. Kemp, 481 U.S. 279 (1987)
McKeiver v. Pennsylvania, 403 U.S. 528 (1971)
McKune v. Lile, 536 U.S. 24 (2002)
Meritor Savings Bank v. Vinson, 477 U.S. 57 (1986)
Miranda v. Arizona, 384 U.S. 436 (1966)
Montana v. Egelhoff, 116 S.Ct. 2013 (1996)
Naidu v. Laird, 539 A.2d 1064 (Del. 1988)
Nassau County v. Arline, 480 U.S. 273, 107 S.Ct. 1123 (1987)
Natanson v. Kline, 186 Kan. 393, 350 P.2d 1093 (1960)
North Carolina v. Alford, 400 U.S. 25, 91 S.Ct. 160 (1970)
O'Connor v. Donaldson, 422 U.S. 563, 95 S.Ct. 2486 (1975)
Olmstead v. L.C., 119 S.Ct. 2176 (1999)
Oncale v. Sundowner Offshore Services, Inc., 118 S.Ct. 998 (1998)
Painter v. Bannister, 258 Iowa 1390, 140 N.W.2d 152 (1966)
Panetti v. Quarterman, 551 U.S. 930 (2007)
Parham v. J.R. and J.L., 442 U.S. 584, 99 S.Ct. 2493 (1979)
Payne v. Tennessee, 111 S.Ct. 2597 (1991)
Peck v. Counseling Service of Addison County, Inc., 146 Vt. 61, 499 A.2d 422 (1985)

Pennsylvania Department of Corrections v. Yeskey, 118 S.Ct. 1952 (1998)
Penry v. Lynaugh, 57 U.S.L.M. 4958 (1989)
People v. Patterson, 39 N.Y.2d 288, 347 N.E.2d 898 (1976)
People v. Shirley, 181 Cal. Rptr. 243 (1982)
People v. Stritzinger, 34 Cal. 3d 505, 668 P.2d 738 (1983)
People v. White, 117 Ca. App.2d 270, 172 Cal. Rptr. 612 (1981)
Planned Parenthood v. Danforth, 428 U.S. 52 (1976)
Powell v. Texas, 392 U.S. 514, 88 S.Ct. 2145 (1968)
Rennie v. Klein, 720 F.2d 266 (3d Cir. 1983)
Riggins v. Nevada, 504 U.S. 127 (1992)
Ring v. Arizona, 536 U.S. 584 (2002)
Robinson v. California, 370 U.S. 660, 82 S.Ct. 1417 (1962)
Rock v. Arkansas, 483 U.S. 44, 107 S.Ct. 2704 (1987)
Rogers v. Commissioner, 390 Mass. 489, 458 N.E.2d 308 (1983)
Roper v. Simmons, 543 U.S. 551 (2005)
Rouse v. Cameron, 125 U.S. App. D.C. 366, 373 F.2d 451 (1966)
Roy v. Hartogs, 381 N.Y.S. 2d 587 (1976)
Santosky v. Kramer, 455 U.S. 745, 102 S.Ct. 1388 (1982)
Schloendorff v. Society of New York Hospital, 105 N.E. 92 (N.Y. 1914)
School Board of Nassau County v. Arline, 480 U.S. 273 (1987)
Sell v. U.S., 539 U.S. 166 (2003)
Sieiling v. Eyman, 478 F.2d 211 (9th Cir. Ariz. 1973)
Specht v. Patterson, 386 U.S. 605, 87 S.Ct. 1209 (1967)
Stanford v. Kentucky, 492 U.S. 361 (1989)
State v. Andring, 342 N.W.2d 128 (Minn. 1984)
State v. Hurd, 173 N.J. Super. 333, 414 A.2d 291 (1980)
State v. Perry, 610 So.2d 746 (La. 1992)
Superintendent of Belchertown State School v. Saikewicz, 373 Mass. 728, 370 N.E.2d
    417 (1977)
Sutton v. United Airlines, Inc., 119 S. Ct. 2139 (1999)
Tarasoff v. Regents, 17 Cal. 3d 425, 551 P.2d 334, 131 Cal. Rptr. 14 (1976)
Thompson v. Oklahoma, 487 U.S. 815 (1988)
Toyota Motor Manufacturing v. Williams, 534 U.S. 184 (2002)
Vacco v. Quill, 117 S.Ct. 2293 (1997)
Vitek v. Jones, 445 U.S. 480, 100 S.Ct. 1254 (1980)
Washington v. Glucksberg, 117 S.Ct. 2258 (1997)
Washington v. Harper, 494 U.S. 210, 110 S.Ct. 1028 (1990)
Washington v. U.S., 129 U.S. App. D.C. 29, 390 F.2d 444 (1967)
Whalen v. Roe, 429 U.S. 589, 97 S.Ct. 869 (1977)
Wickline v. State, 192 Cal. App. 3d 1630, 239 Cal. Rptr. 810 (1987)
Wilson v. U.S., 129 U.S. App. D.C. 107, 391 F.2d 460 (1968)
Wyatt v. Stickney, 344 F.Supp. 387 (M.D. Ala. 1972)
Youngberg v. Romeo, 457 U.S. 307, 102 S.Ct. 2452 (1982)
Zinermon v. Burch, 494 U.S. 113, 110 S.Ct. 975 (1990)

General references

Abrams, A.A. 2010. Competencies in Civil Law. In *Textbook of Forensic Psychiatry*, 2nd Edition (Edited by Simon, R.I., Gold, L.H.), 241–243. Washington, DC: American Psychiatric Publishing.

American Academy of Psychiatry and the Law. May 2005. Ethics Guidelines for the Practice of Forensic Psychiatry. Available at http://www.aapl.org/ethics.htm (last accessed September 18, 2014).

American Board of Psychiatry and Neurology. n.d. Application Materials. http://www.abpn.com/ifas_fp.html (last accessed September 22, 2014).

American Board of Psychiatry and Neurology. n.d. Forensic Psychiatry. http://www.abpn.com/sub_fp.html (last accessed August 30, 2014).

American Board of Psychiatry and Neurology. n.d. Homepage. http://www.abpn.com/ (last accessed September 26, 2014).

American Medical Association. 2008. *Guides to the Evaluation of Permanent Impairment*, 6th Edition (Edited by Rondinelli, R.D.). Chicago, IL: American Medical Association.

American Psychiatric Association. 2000. *Psychiatric Services in Jails and Prisons*, 2nd Edition. Washington, DC: APA Press.

Appelbaum, P.S. 1997. A theory of ethics for forensic psychiatry. *Journal of the American Academy of Psychiatry and the Law*, 25:233–247.

Behnke, S., Hilliard, J. 1998. *The Essentials of Massachusetts Mental Health Law*. Norton & Company.

Binder, L.M. 1990. Malingering following minor head trauma. *Clinical Neuropsychologist*, 4:25–36.

Bradford, J., Booth, B., Seto, M.C. 2010. Forensic Assessment of Sex Offenders. In *Textbook of Forensic Psychiatry*, 2nd Edition (Edited by Simon, R.I., Gold, L.H.), 383–385. Washington, DC: American Psychiatric Publishing.

Brown, B.M. 1977. An examinee's perspective on board certification. *American Journal of Psychiatry*, 134:1261–1264.

Ciccone, J.R., Jones, J. 2010. Personal Injury Litigation and Forensic Psychiatric Assessment. In *Textbook of Forensic Psychiatry*, 2nd Edition (Edited by Simon, R.I., Gold, L.H.), 261–281. Washington, DC: American Psychiatric Publishing.

Cunnien, A.J. 1997. Psychiatric and Medical Syndromes Associated with Deception. In *Clinical Assessment of Malingering and Deception*, 2nd Edition (Edited by Rogers, R.), 23–46. New York: Guilford Press.

Daniel, A.E. 2006. Preventing suicide in prison: A collaborative responsibility of administration, custodial and clinical staff. *Journal of the American Academy of Psychiatry and the Law*, 34:165–175.

Drukteinis, A.M. 2010. Disability. In *Textbook of Forensic Psychiatry*, 2nd Edition (Edited by Simon, R.I., Gold, L.H.), 285–288. Washington, DC: American Psychiatric Publishing.

Dusky v. U.S., 362 U.S. 402, 80 S.Ct. 788 (1960).

Ford v. Wainwright, 106 S.Ct. 2595 (1986).

Gold, L.H. 2010. The Workplace. In *Textbook of Forensic Psychiatry*, 2nd Edition (Edited by Simon, R.I., Gold, L.H.), 303–334. Washington, DC: American Psychiatric Publishing.

Green, P. 2003. *Word Memory Test*. Edmonton, Alberta, Canada: Green's Publishing.

Grisso, T. 2003. *Evaluating Competencies: Forensic Assessments and Instruments*, 2nd Edition. New York: Kluwer Academic.

Grisso, T., Appelbaum, P.S. 1995. Comparison of standards for assessing patients' capacities to make treatment decisions. *American Journal of Psychiatry*, 152:1033–1037.

Grisso, T., Appelbaum, P.S. 1998. *Assessing Competence to Consent to Treatment*. New York and Oxford: Oxford University Press.

Gutheil, T.G. 2009. *The Psychiatrist as Expert Witness*, 2nd Edition. Washington, DC: American Psychiatric Publishing.

Gutheil, T.G. 2010. Forensic Ethics. In *American Academy of Psychiatry and the Law, Forensic Psychiatry Review Course*. Presented at the annual meeting, Tucson, AZ.

Gutheil, T.G. 2010. Sexual Harassment. In *American Academy of Psychiatry and the Law, Forensic Psychiatry Review Course*. Presented at the annual meeting, Tucson, AZ.

Gutheil, T.G., Appelbaum, P.S., Wexler, D.B. 1983. The inappropriateness of "least restrictive alternative" analysis for involuntary procedures with the institutionalized mentally ill. *Journal of Psychiatry and Law*, 11:7–17.

Hare, R.D. 1991. *The Hare Psychopathy Checklist–Revised*. Toronto, Ontario: Multi-Health Systems.

Hare, R.D., Clark, D., Grann, M., et al. 2000. Psychopathy and the predictive validity of the PCL-R: An international perspective. *Behavioral Sciences and the Law*, 18(5):623–645.

Hathaway, S.R., McKinley, J.C. 1989. *The Minnesota Multiphasic Personality Inventory-2*. Minneapolis, MN: University of Minnesota Press.

Heilbrun, K., Radelet, M., Dvoskin, J. 1992. The debate on treating individuals incompetent for execution. *American Journal of Psychiatry*, 149:5.

Knoll, J.L. 2010. Ethics in Forensic Psychiatry. In *Textbook of Forensic Psychiatry*, 2nd Edition (Edited by Simon, R.I., Gold, L.H.), 118–119. Washington, DC: American Psychiatric Publishing.

LeBourgeois, H.W., Thompson, J.W., Black, F.W. 2010. Malingering. In *Textbook of Forensic Psychiatry*, 2nd Edition (Edited by Simon, R.I., Gold, L.H.), 468–469. Washington, DC: American Psychiatric Publishing.

M'Naghten's Case, 8 Eng. Rep. 718, 8 Eng. Rep. 722 (1843)

Maleson, F.G., Fink, P.J., Field, H.L. 1980. Board certification anxiety. *American Journal of Psychiatry*, 137:837–840.

Melton, G.B., Petrila, J., Poythress, N.G., Slobogin, C. 1997. Compensating mental injuries: Worker's compensation and torts. In *Psychological Evaluation for the Courts, a Handbook for Mental Health Professionals and Lawyers*, 2nd Edition, 401–413. New York: Guilford Press.

Melton, G.B., Petrila, J., Poythress, N.G., et al. 1997. *Psychological Evaluations for the Courts: A Handbook for Mental Health Professionals and Lawyers*, 2nd Edition New York: Guilford Press.

Metzner, J.L., Buck, J.B. 2000. Psychiatric Disability Determinations and Personal Injury Litigation. In *Principles and Practice of Forensic Psychiatry*, 2nd Edition (Edited by Rosner, R.), 260–272. Boca Raton, FL: CRC Press.

Metzner, J.L., Dvoskin, J.A. 2010. Correctional Psychiatry. In *Textbook of Forensic Psychiatry*, 2nd Edition (Edited by Simon, R.I., Gold, L.H.). Washington, DC: American Psychiatric Publishing.

Meyer, D.J., Simon, R.I., Shuman, D.W. 2010. Professional Liability in Psychiatric Practice and Requisite Standard of Care. In *Textbook of Forensic Psychiatry*, 2nd Edition (Edited by Simon, R.I., Gold, L.H.), 208–220. Washington, DC: American Psychiatric Publishing.

Miller, R.D. 2000. Criminal Competence. In *Principles and Practice of Forensic Psychiatry*, 2nd Edition (Edited by Rosner, R.), 202–206. Boca Raton, FL: CRC Press.

Miller, R.D. 2000. Criminal Responsibility. In *Principles and Practice of Forensic Psychiatry*, 2nd Edition (Edited by Rosner, R.), 221–225. Boca Raton, FL: CRC Press.

Miller, H. 2001. *Miller Forensic Assessment of Symptoms Test (M-FAST). Professional Manual*. Lutz, FL: Psychological Assessment Resources.

Morrison, J., Munoz, R.A. 2009. *Boarding Time: The Psychiatry Candidate's New Guide to Part II of the ABPN Examination*, 4th Edition. Washington, DC: American Psychiatric Publishing.

Mossman, D. 2010. Understanding Risk Assessment Instruments. In *Textbook of Forensic Psychiatry*, 2nd Edition (Edited by Simon, R.I., Gold, L.H.), 563–581. Washington, DC: American Psychiatric Publishing.

Office of Justice Programs. n.d. SORNA. http://ojp.gov/smart/sorna.htm (last accessed September 16, 2014).

Pear, R. 2009. Justices' rule in discrimination case may draw quick action by Obama. *New York Times*, January 5. Available at http://www.nytimes.com/2009/01/05/us/politics/05rights.htm (last accessed September 16, 2014).

Perlin, M.L., Champine, P., Dlugacz, H.A., Connell, M. 2008. *Competence in the Law: From Legal Theory to Application*. John Wiley & Sons.

Peterson, L.E.I., Blackburn, B., King, M.R. 2014. Completing self-assessment modules during residency is associated with better certification exam results. *Family Medicine*, 46(8):597–602.

Pinals, D.A. 2010. Criminal Competencies. In *American Academy of Psychiatry and the Law, Forensic Psychiatry Review Course*. Presented at the annual meeting, Tucson, AZ.

Pinals, D.A., Frierson, R.L. 2014. The educational mission in forensic publishing. *Journal of the American Academy of Psychiatry and the Law*, 42(3):290–296.

Poythress, N.G., Bonnie, R.J., Hoge, S.K., et al. 1994. Client abilities to assist counsel and make decisions in criminal cases: Findings from three studies. *Law and Human Behavior*, 18(4):437–452.

Prison Rape Elimination Act. 2003. http://www.prearesourcecenter.org/about/prison-rape-elimination-act-prea (last accessed September 25, 2014).

Prisoner Litigation Reform Act (PLRA). n.d. https://www.aclu.org/sites/default/files/images/asset_upload_file79_25805.pdf (last accessed September 2014).

Prosono, M. 2000. History of Forensic Psychiatry. In *Principles and Practice of Forensic Psychiatry*, 2nd Edition (Edited by Rosner, R.). Boca Raton, FL: CRC Press.

Reeves, R., Rosner, R. 2000. Education and Training in Forensic Psychiatry. In *Principles and Practice of Forensic Psychiatry*, 2nd Edition (Edited by Rosner, R.), 52–55. Boca Raton, FL: CRC Press.

Resnick, P.J. 1999. The detection of malingered psychosis. *Psychiatric Clinics of North America*, 22:159–172.

Resnick, P.J. 2000. Guidelines for Courtroom Testimony. In *Principles and Practice of Forensic Psychiatry*, 2nd Edition (Edited by Rosner, R.), 38. Boca Raton, FL: CRC Press.

Resnick, P.J. 2010. The Detection of Malingered Mental Illness. In *American Academy of Psychiatry and the Law, Forensic Psychiatry Review Course*. Presented at the annual meeting, Tucson, AZ.

Resnick, P.J., Knoll, J. 2005. Faking it: How to detect malingered psychosis. *Current Psychiatry*, 4(11):13–25.

Resnick, P.J., Knoll, J.L. 2008. Malingered Psychosis. In *Clinical Assessment of Malingering*, 2nd Edition (Edited by Rogers, R.), 51–68. New York: Guilford Press.

Resnick, P.J., West, S., Payne, J.W. 2008. Malingering of Posttraumatic Disorders. In *Clinical Assessment of Malingering and Deception*, 3rd Edition (Edited by Rogers, R.), 111–112. New York: Guilford Press.

Resnick, P.J. 2010. Basic Law for Psychiatrists. In *American Academy of Psychiatry and the Law, Forensic Psychiatry Review Course*. Presented at the annual meeting, Tucson, AZ.

Resnick P.J., Gutheil, T., Pinals, D.A., Scott, C.L. 2010. *American Academy of Psychiatry and the Law, Forensic Psychiatry Review Course*. Presented at the annual meeting, Tucson, AZ.

Rice, M.E., Harris, G.T., Quinsey, V.L. 2002. The appraisal of violence risk. *Current Opinion in Psychiatry* 15(6):589–593.

Rogers, R., Bagby, R.M., Dickens, S.E. 1992. *Structured Interview of Reported Symptoms (SIRS)*. Lutz, FL: Psychological Assessment Resources.

Rogers, R., Sewell, K.W., Morey, L.C., et al. 1996. Detection of feigned mental disorder on the personality assessment inventory: A discriminant analysis. *Journal of Personality Assessment*, 67:629–640.

Rosner, R. (ed.) 2000. *Principles and Practice of Forensic Psychiatry*, 2nd Edition. Boca Raton, FL: CRC Press.

Roth, L.K., Meisel, A. 1977. Dangerousness, confidentiality and the duty to warn. *American Journal of Psychiatry*, 134:508–511.

Schwartz, H.I., Mack, D.M., Zeman, P.M. 2000. Hospitalization: Voluntary and Involuntary. In *Principles and Practice of Forensic Psychiatry*, 2nd Edition (Edited by Rosner, R.), 108–120. Boca Raton, FL: CRC Press.

Scott, C.L. 2010. The Americans with Disabilities Act amendments of 2008. Implications for the forensic psychiatrist. *Journal of American Academy Psychiatry and the Law*, 38:95–99.

Scott, C.L. 2010. Child Abuse & Psychic Harm and Worker's Compensation. In *American Academy of Psychiatry and the Law, Forensic Psychiatry Review Course*. Presented at the annual meeting, Tucson, AZ.

Scott, C.L. 2010. Child Custody & Correctional Psychiatry & Psychiatry and the Death Penalty. In *American Academy of Psychiatry and the Law, Forensic Psychiatry Review Course*. Presented at the annual meeting, Tucson, AZ.

Scott, C.L. 2010. Competency to Stand Trial and the Insanity Defense. In *Textbook of Forensic Psychiatry*, 2nd Edition (Edited by Simon, R.I., Gold, L.H.), 337–371. Washington, DC: American Psychiatric Publishing.

Scott, C.L. 2010. Psychiatry and the Death Penalty & Psychic Harm and Workers' Comp & Sexual Offenders and the Law. In *American Academy of Psychiatry and the Law, Forensic Psychiatry Review Course*. Presented at the annual meeting, Tucson, AZ.

Shore, J.H., Scheiber, S.C. 1994. *Certification, Recertification and Lifetime Learning*. Washington, DC: American Psychiatric Association.

Simon, R.I., Gold, L.H. (eds.) 2010. *Textbook of Forensic Psychiatry*, 2nd Edition. Washington, DC: American Psychiatric Publishing.

Silva, J.A., Weinstock, R., Leong, G.B. 2000. Forensic Report Writing. In *Principles and Practice of Forensic Psychiatry*, 2nd Edition (Edited by Rosner, R.), 31–36. Boca Raton, FL: CRC Press.

Slick, D., Hopp, G., Strauss, E., et al. 1997. *Victoria Symptom Validity Test Professional Manual*. Lutz, FL: Psychological Assessment Resources.

Tombaugh, T.N. 1996. *The Test of Memory Malingering*. Toronto, Ontario, Canada: Multi-Health Systems.

U.S. Congress, House. 1992. The Constitution of the United States of America, As Amended, H. Doc. 102–188, 102nd Cong., 2nd sess. Washington, DC: GPO.

Weinstock, R., Leong, G.B., Silva, J.A. 2000. Defining Forensic Psychiatry: Roles and Responsibilities. In *Principles and Practice of Forensic Psychiatry*, 2nd Edition (Edited by Rosner, R.). Boca Raton, FL: CRC Press.

West, S., Noffsinger, S.G. 2006. Is this patient competent to stand trial? *Current Psychiatry*, 5(6):36–41.

West, S., Noffsinger, S.G. 2006. Is this patient not guilty by reason of insanity? *Current Psychiatry*, 5(8):54–62.

Wettstein, R.M. 2000. Specific Issues in Psychiatric Malpractice. In *Principles and Practice of Forensic Psychiatry*, 2nd Edition (Edited by Rosner, R.), 250. Boca Raton, FL: CRC Press.

Index